THE YEAR OFF

The Anti-Budget Solution to Mastering Your
Money and Following Your Dreams

Steve Larsen

The Year Off
The Anti-Budget Solution to Mastering Your Money and Following Your Dreams

© 2020 by Steve Larsen

Produced by Raab & Co. | Raabandco.com

ISBN: 978-1-7353664-0-1
eISBN: 978-1-7353664-1-8

Table of Contents

Introduction

"I just feel so trapped."

It was our second meeting, and we were reviewing the money plan I had just developed for Justin and his wife. We had covered retirement, insurance, taxes, and all those other boring topics, and we were finally moving on to something that mattered: Why was he continuing to work at a job he didn't like?

"I need to get a few things paid off while I wait for my pension to kick in," Justin explained. "Then I can find something else to do."

Justin was a teacher, and, like many educators, he found himself frustrated by the system. He wanted to leave and try something else, but it was the only adult job he'd ever had and the only type of work he felt he knew how to do. He couldn't see how leaving could ever be an option.

"So to summarize," I said, "you are going to piss away 10 to 15 percent of your adult life doing something you don't enjoy anymore?"

"Easy for you to say," he replied. "I have bills, a spouse, and people depending on me. It's not like I can just drop everything and figure something else out." He looked at me like I had three heads. "I can't live in a fantasy land."

"Actually," I told him, "you can live right here in the real world and *still* find a way to enjoy the five or six years of your life that you are about ready to give up on."

He gave me a skeptical look. "Okay, I'll bite. What is this secret that can change my fortunes?"

"It's not a secret," I explained. "It's a *system*. A simple system that helps you to climb out of whatever hole you feel you are stuck in. As a matter of fact, I'm about to use it to climb out of one myself and explore ideas I've wanted to for years."

This time, Justin seemed intrigued. I leaned back in my chair, thinking about the projects I was excited to pursue over the course of my own upcoming year off. I knew my system could help him do the same.

"Here's how to start."

There *Is* a Way Out

As a personal financial planner for nearly twenty years, I have seen too many clients like Justin: unhappy in their jobs, longing for something else, but absolutely convinced they couldn't have it—because of, they assumed, money.

But taking time off from your job is not a fantasy. *Your money doesn't have to control your life.*

Over the years, I've developed a solution, a simple way for you to organize your money so you know exactly where it's going each month and don't overspend. After taking a few simple steps to calculate your needs, you can use this same system to actually take time off. To get away from your job. To figure out what you want from your life. And best of all, there's no budgeting involved (really!).

No longer do you have to feel trapped between a paycheck and a dream. The solution to getting your life train on a track you love is here within these pages. It can happen for me, it can happen for Justin, and I know it can happen for you.

Why This System Works

Let's face it: Money can be emotional and difficult. Even those who are good with money can find it an overwhelming and emotional topic.

Most books on this topic throw a bunch of big ideas at you, then expect you to build, manage, and maintain the entire system on your own, leaving you floundering under your spreadsheets and Starbucks receipts. Talk about overwhelming! No wonder so many budgets fail. (Maybe it's not you that's the problem . . .)

With the Year Off Money System I've developed, you won't drown under words like "retirement" and "financial responsibility" or even "financial freedom." We are after freedom, all right, but not monetary freedom.

This is your first step toward freeing yourself from the doubts, worries, and fears that plague you every day and keep you from a life of meaning. You *can* take the time for yourself to build a life of meaning. And best of all, you can do it *without a budget*.

The Year Off Money System—or YO System, as it's known throughout this book—will put your ducks in a row so you can climb out of the rut race, take an entire year for yourself, and move in any direction you want, during and after your time off: new career, nonprofit or volunteer work, starting a business, exploring new hobbies, rebuilding relationships—whatever it is you need to live a more fulfilling life.

How This Book Is Structured

In this book, we'll work through the two main challenges that lie between you and a life of freedom: figuring out what to do with your time off and setting up a system for your money to make it possible. With actionable advice, step-by-step instructions, and valuable worksheets designed to get your house in order, you'll be starting your adventure sooner than you thought!

I've put all you need to know into the YO System behind this book. And it's easier than you think.

Each chapter will focus on one of two goals for kickstarting your twelve months of freedom: planning what to do and setting up your money. Chapters that focus on planning what to do are marked with a lightbulb ( ) icon, while chapters that work through the money system are marked with a moneybag ( ) icon.

In Chapter 1 ( ), you'll learn new ways to reframe your attitude toward money and your own desires and values that are crucial in getting your YO System off the ground.

Just as importantly, in Chapter 2 ( ), you'll look at your own strengths, experiences, and goals to determine exactly what you might want to do with your year off so that your time can be meaningful and impactful, for you and for the world.

In Chapters 3 and 4 (🏠), you will learn a new approach to daily financial management (no budgeting here!) and take stock of your current finances. Looking at your money, warts and all, can be intimidating, but I promise, it only gets better from here. You simply have to understand what is going on in order to fix it.

In Chapter 5 (🏠), you are going to calculate how far away your escape date is. The answer you get will be both exciting and scary, but remember, it's only a number (and we'll look at ways to shrink that number).

In Chapter 6 (💡), you will address the skills you need to develop to build toward a successful break from your regular life. You likely will have some waiting time. The habits and routines you focus on now will determine how successful you are in finding—and implementing—year off activities worthy of your time.

In Chapter 7 (🏠), I'll share tips for cutting that number in half or even more. Through simple strategies, you'll be able to leverage the power of the YO System to shave months or even years from your year off date.

In Chapter 8 (🏠), I'll help you set up your safety net and arrange your affairs so you're free to pursue your new future worry-free.

Finally, in Chapter 9, you'll learn how to live a life without regret.

With an abundance of practical exercises, real-world advice, and actionable steps to help you implement the system for yourself, the system described in *The Year Off* will guide you every step of the way.

Freedom Is Closer Than You Thought

If you are living paycheck to paycheck, then you are living without freedom. You are living a reactive life, letting outside events dictate what you can and can't do, who you can and can't be. And you are living in an uncertain future. And that often means you are living without meaning, because you can't do what you want to do.

Change can be scary, but if you were curious enough to crack open this book, you are ready to do this. You can flip your insecurities the bird and choose to live your life on your terms. If you feel nervous, just keep reading. Follow my system, and you will get there. Many people before you already have.

I should know. I'm one of them.

Today, I no longer let my job and my bank account tell me what is possible. By putting my career and my money to work to support the way I want my life to be, instead of the other way around, *I* determine what I do to achieve personal satisfaction and make an impact in the world. And I kickstarted all of it by making the decision to invest in myself, my loved ones, and my future by taking a year off.

Say yes to freedom. The Year Off Money System will help you get proactive and set your money up to flow smoothly and accumulate faster while you decide how much time to take off. Find a deeper purpose in your life. Live intentionally, the way you want to live. Discover, being who you want to be.

My intention is for this book to help you build the personal and monetary habits you need to continually move toward being the person you want to be, all while accumulating enough funds to experience one year of personal freedom and discovery. I believe these financial and other habits can change your mental and even physical well-being, and a year outside your current daily routine can give you important perspective for what you want out of your future. By the end of this book, you will have a smoothly working money system, a solid plan for your time off, and the habits to get you where you want to go.

Now is the time to live intentionally, because you don't get another shot at this life. *The Year Off* will give you the tools—and the permission—to finally give yourself the freedom you need to build the life you really want.

CHAPTER 1

Escaping the Rut Race

In college, I was long on idealism and short on brainpower. I remember sitting in my dorm room with my roommate, drinking beer and talking about how immensely we were going to change the world. The question for us wasn't *whether* the world would bend to our will, it was *how far* it would bend.

Think globally, act locally! We are the world! Reduce, reuse, recycle! Buy the world a Coke! We were going to do *all* of it. What would future generations do after we two solved all the world's problems? We were going to make these changes happen whether the world was ready for them or not.

I gave it my best shot. First, I stayed up late drinking almost every night in college, talking about how much of an impact I was going to have. That was a good start, I guess. Then I got my first real job and started putting money into the Salvation Army kettles at Christmas time. Then I bought new clothes and new furniture for my new apartment and took my old stuff to Goodwill. I thought for sure donating my heavily used brown couch—which started out white—and a pair of jorts would start to turn things around for society. It didn't. I was dejected by this cruel reality that nobody wanted my homemade jorts.

As I entered my thirties, my business was starting to make money, and I had real-life skills to offer, so I joined a few nonprofit boards and hit the dinner fundraising circuit. To my amazement, giving financial advice to snooty social clubs and getting drunk at $100 charity dinners didn't seem to change the world much after all.

Approaching my forties, I knew something had to change. I wanted to get *involved*. I wanted to donate my time and talents—not just my money—to something that mattered. I found five nonprofits that were making a difference and offered to do anything I could to help, from accounting services to assisting on a soup line.

Not one of them took me up on my offer. Turns out a lot of people are trying to change the world in the same small ways.

At my ripe old age of thirty-nine, I found that my natural spirit of wonder and optimism had dried out, crusted over, and shrunk into a permanent lump of disappointment. The unlimited potential that my roommate and I had been prepared to tap had dissipated. I was feeling very disappointed that I hadn't done more with my life, and I was terrified I wouldn't accomplish anything else. But how could I at this stage? I had a full-time job and a family! I had to work. I had to earn. I had to save money for the future! How could I overcome these excuses for my procrastination? I was doomed to my own hellish version of *Groundhog Day*.

Of course, as it turns out, I wasn't stuck at all. And neither are you.

In this chapter, you'll learn why you feel so stuck, the forces that keep us from breaking free of our routines, and new ways to reframe your attitude toward money and your own desires and values. This important transformation is critical to using the Year Off Money System to take control of your own finances and refocus your future.

Why We're Stuck in the Rut Race

That isn't a typo; I do mean *rut race*. A *rat race* is being stuck in a cage, playing stupid games to win stupid prizes by someone else's design. But we're not rats, and no one put us in this race. We backed right into our very own cages. We did this to ourselves.

Being stuck in the rut race means mindlessly following the well-worn path before you—the one you wore down for yourself—until one day you wake up and five years have passed you by.

We don't jump into the rut race all at once, but step by step, until we can't see a life beyond the daily grooves we have created for ourselves. First, we get a job and become accustomed to a certain lifestyle. Then, we take out a mortgage, buy cars and boats, and develop a taste for travel and eating out. But now we have to keep working to make the payments. We became chained to our desks—or more accurately, chained to our debts, chained to the income on our W2s.

So why do many of us still feel stuck? Over the years, I have found that people who believe they are at the mercy of their paycheck tend to be stuck in one of five ruts. Do you recognize any of these scenarios?

- **Scenario 1: The Dying Dream.** You started out with big plans, but now you're working a job you don't like, pushing through to see whether that next promotion or upward career move solves your unease. You want to do something different, but it's so hard to turn your back on all the seniority and skills you have built up . . . even if your career wasn't ever your first choice, and even if you've never really let go of your original dreams.

- **Scenario 2: Stuck in Debt.** At the time, it really seemed like you needed that new kitchen, boat, or vacation. Maybe the payment increase looked minimal at first, but now, too much debt is weighing you down. You've debated blowing the whole thing up in bankruptcy and starting over, but you've opted to do things the right way, to put in more years of hard work and slowly burn down your debt.

- **Scenario 3: Disappearing Dinero.** You're making a great salary, more than ever before, yet the money disappears every month (even if you earn well into six figures), and you feel forced to keep making more of it. Maybe you've tried to get your spending habits under control before—or worse, you attempted the painful process of creating and following a *budget*—but you gave up. (It's shocking how easy it is to spend money and forget what you bought. Did you really need it if you can't remember buying it?) Now, even with raises and bonuses, the money still disappears before you can really make it count.

- **Scenario 4: Unhelpful Financial Help.** Maybe you tried to get a handle on your money before by reading a few books or even hiring an advisor. But it either didn't help or it made things worse. Many folks have been burned by financial "advice." The financial advisor industry is rife with pirates who will take your money and feed you advice they found lying on the floor (or in an email from management, who wants them to sell you certain products). My first book was all about how to avoid these well-camouflaged scams.

- **Scenario 5: Stuck Under Sunk Costs.** Many of my clients think they have too much already invested in the path they have chosen for it to make sense to shift now. This belief is called the *sunk cost fallacy*, where we continue a behavior because of a previous investment of time, money, or effort. When you convince yourself that going in a different direction doesn't make sense because you've "put too much into this," it's hard to conceive of how different (and awesome) life could be if you made a radical change. Thinking you are beholden to your efforts of the past will only keep you stuck and unhappy, sinking more time and costs into the fallacy.

These are just some of the lies we tell ourselves to keep us in the race. Maybe you recognize your own familiar refrain. But as it turns out, the only thing stopping us from climbing out is our own fear.

If you do see yourself in any of these situations, something needs to change. Your future depends on it.

Change Your Perspective, Change Your Future

The thing about the rut race is that when you're stuck in it, none of it feels self-imposed. Why would anyone do such a thing? But for each of these unpleasant scenarios above that you might find yourself in, there's a lie that you've decided to believe. You don't have to feel hopeless; you just need a new perspective.

- **It's Okay to Want More**

  Most people I've seen—and I'll use Gen Xers like me as an example—hit their late thirties or forties and just start wanting to do something new and different. This shift is completely natural. As a society, we need to make it normal to take a year or so off midcareer for exploration and a lifestyle reset. Who says sabbaticals are only for academics? Let's bring them into style for the mainstream, starting with you! (Just please leave the tweed jackets at the door.)

- **Debt Is Not a Life Sentence**

  If you've resigned yourself to a life of debt and obligation, think again! With another look at your money situation, you may be able to pay down your debt faster than you think and *still* manage to take some time off. Better yet, maybe you don't have to wait until your debt is gone to enjoy the life you crave. You just need a way to see the big picture and stay on top of it all (and, in the future, decide more accurately whether you can take on more debt).

- **You Can Say Goodbye to Budgeting**

  If you have attempted torturing yourself by budgeting or some other money-managing system, you know how most of them don't work. It's not you! Budgeting is fundamentally flawed (and yes, that's a CPA telling you that!). Instead, my YO System will show you a simple way to arrange your money accounts to put you well on your way to corralling and tracking your money, plus doing something meaningful and lasting with it. As a bonus, you can look in one place and instantly see what you can afford to spend.

- **It Is Possible to Control Your Financial Destiny**

I know that when getting help doesn't go well, the experience can be traumatizing and have lasting effects. I understand why the experience might have made you skeptical of yet another "financial help" book, and I understand the urge to avoid the whole unpleasant situation. That's just psychology. But this book is different. Not only are you going to get your money set up to flow well, but you will be able to leverage it to earn some powerful time off. The YO System will allow you to manage your money with ease and buy you less stress. If you do the exercises, use my step-by-step instructions to streamline your own finances, and keep following the system, it will simplify your financial life *approaching* your year off, *during* your year off, and *for the rest of your life.*

- **Sunk Costs Are an Illusion**

What sunk costs are you avoiding walking away from? Is your daily lack of happiness and fulfillment more expensive than those costs? Are you ready to take a break and do what you've been longing to do? When I took my own break, I left behind my undergraduate business degree (four years and $40,000), my master's degree (two years and $20,000), my CPA license (one year, $3,000, and four super-hard tests), and my CFP certification (one year, $2,000, and another super-hard test). All sunk costs. That money is spent, no matter what I do next, and I don't owe it anything.

When you can look the lie in the face and call it what it is, you can break its hold on you and move forward with your life. It's true what they say: the truth really can set you free.

Who Do You Really Want to Be?

What if the answer to your nagging doubts isn't what, but *who*? Our brains naturally focus on what we want, what we need, what our goals are, and what will make us happy. I'm guessing you have experienced the same thing that I have—the "whats" never end, because there is always another one to pursue. If you have been working your tail off for a promotion, you will probably get it eventually. Then you will feel great for a week before shifting your focus to the next "what" that will finally make you happy. "Now that I am a VP, I need a vacation property!"

In the end, though, it's just stuff and fluff. What if the answer to living with purpose is discovering *who* you want to be? *Who* are you overlooking that could really use your help? *Who* do you want a better relationship with? *Who* are you wishing you could be right now?

When I finally let myself think about a life of freedom, everything started to change for me. After years of working hard through the ups and downs of the financial advice industry, everything was beginning to come together. I was contacted by three other financial planners who loved what I was building and decided to join me. My business revenues were growing by over 50 percent per year. I crossed the $100 million mark in assets managed for my clients (a major milestone in the investment business). My employees were growing into their roles every day and practically managing themselves. The future was bright, and my firm was primed for even more growth moving forward. This all happened in the span of a year, the same year I turned forty.

With nothing but clear sailing ahead to grow my business into elite levels in my region, the Pacific Northwest, I did something crazy. I did the only thing I've *really* wanted to do for the last fifteen years or so: I took a year off to try something new.

I decided to throw myself into writing a book—this book—to help as many people as I could to also do something meaningful with their lives. It's my goal that this radical change will create benefits in my life, in my family, and in the world that far exceed what I left behind me.

Instead of angling for a promotion at work, what if you angled to be a person who checks in with their entire department every week to see what you can do to help? What if you became a person who's focused on supporting other people's successes? Two things would happen. First, you would get that promotion a hell of a lot faster. And second, *you would be a person who helps other people*. That isn't a short-term victory that will fade away like your glorious promotion will; it's a long-term change that will motivate you to get up every Monday and start your week being a "you" that you enjoy.

How does who you are right now compare to who you want to be? Who are you, really, behind those cheerful selfies? The Year Off Money System isn't just about money. From now until your time off, figuring this out is your goal, and this book will help you reach it.

Nothing in life is permanent—not jobs, not interests, not relationships. After working in one industry for a while, it's natural and pretty common to want to switch and do something else, maybe even something radically different. You are never too far down any path to pivot toward what you were meant to do. You just have to allow yourself to hope.

One Last Thing: Find an Accountability Partner

Your year off journey will affect the people around you. When the time is right, you should talk through your ideas with your spouse, friends, family, or anyone else you know will be supportive.

On top of that, it's important to find one buddy—your accountability partner—to hold you accountable to all the steps in this book, to anchor you in your intentions. Your accountability partner should:

- Be someone you trust, someone you can share your money numbers with
- Be someone who shoots it to you straight at all times
- Keep you pumped up and positive
- Be willing and responsible enough to show up to regular check-ins with you (beverages may be involved)

Find an accountability partner who is committed to being there with you for every exercise in this book and every step of the way. (I've provided checklists at the end of each chapter to make this process nice and easy.)

Remember that the people around you want to see you happy,

but not everyone loves change. Be gentle with those folks. Misery loves company, and if you start to enjoy yourself too much, some may attempt to bring you back down to their level. That's fine; if others don't want to come with you, that's their choice. Just keep on top of your plans with your accountability partner, and remember that this journey is for you—for your happiness, your health, and your ability to make the biggest impact possible in the world!

The only barrier to a better life is your money fear, inexperience, and doubt stopping you from taking control of your financial situation. Stopping you from looking at your (possibly disorganized) accounts. From moving money around and adding things up to get the number you need. From mastering your money and doing the work.

You stand on the threshold of being able to take a year off and change your life. Are you ready to allow yourself the freedom to live a more meaningful life?

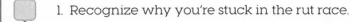
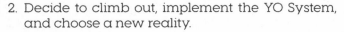

Chapter 1 Accountability
CHECKLIST

Starting Out!

1. Recognize why you're stuck in the rut race.

2. Decide to climb out, implement the YO System, and choose a new reality.

Think Freedom

3. Start thinking about the person you'd become if you had the time and freedom to follow your dreams.

Accountability Partner

4. Speak with a potential accountability partner (your "AP"), and get their buy-in. Commit to being accountability partners and set a time to meet regularly.

5. The name of the person I select to hold me accountable while I prepare for my year off is

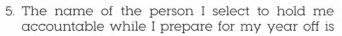

_____.

CHAPTER 2

What to Do With Your Year Off

A couple years ago, every day at work felt like a grind for me, and I would occasionally end up at my local watering hole afterward. My friend Jared, a medical device sales manager, would often fill the barstool next to me.

One night, before heading out, Jared sold me on one more drink, as he often does. He happened to be avoiding getting home too early for dinner with his in-laws. I understand that pain, so I decided to kill some time by spilling the beans about my plan to take an entire year off.

Jared looked at me in disbelief. "Why fourteen months?" he asked. I could tell Jared thought for sure I was making that number up. I grabbed the nearest cocktail napkin that I hadn't spilled on and started mapping out the money side of it. I knew exactly what it cost me to live every month, so twelve times that was how much I needed in the bank to afford the time away from my work.

Next, I laid out exactly how long it would take to save that much money: fourteen months. In just over a year, I told him, I would have enough money set aside to take one full year off from work and do whatever I want.

Whatever. I. Want.

"I'm in," he told me immediately, and we gleefully flipped the napkin and proceeded to calculate Jared's prospects. He was looking at nineteen months: not too bad for a guy who didn't even know it was possible until five minutes earlier.

Then he fell silent, looking at the bar. I could tell something was bothering him. I picked up the pencil to run the numbers again, bracing myself for his disbelief that such a thing could be possible.

But that wasn't what was on his mind. Finally, Jared asked me, "But what the heck would I *do* with all that time?"

I paused, pencil hovering in midair. It was a very good question—but I couldn't give him the answer. I could only help him crunch the numbers. To really find his true purpose in the world, Jared had to truly look inside himself and ask some hard questions about where he was and where he wanted to be.

"That I can't answer for you," I said, clapping him on the shoulder. "But you have nineteen months to figure it out."

If taking a year off in the middle of your life were a simple thing you could pull off on a whim, you would have done it already. In reality, this is a major life change that takes planning and discipline. You need to have a complete grasp of where your money is going while developing a plan for how to manage yourself during the time you're not working, so you don't spend twelve months binging on Fig Newtons and *Friends* reruns. And that's exactly what I will teach you throughout this book. First, however, you need to start considering the answer to one core question: What would you *do* with your time off?

If you are like me, you can think of many cool things you would *like* to do and see during your time away . . . but I'm a little hazy on how sitting on a beach every day with a tasty beverage or three will help you fulfill your purpose or make the world a better place.

Coming up with a list of awesome experiences that only benefit *you* is called *daydreaming*. But this isn't a daydream; this is reality. Putting together ideas for sharing your unique talents with others or taking on a learning experience that makes you a better person is called *living intentionally.*

If you are lucky, you already have some good ideas for what to do on your year off. If you don't have the answer today, then let's start looking for it! Finding your purpose in the world is not an instant process. It's something that has to be considered over time.

The goal of this chapter is to get you brainstorming all the things you would like to experience and ways you could be impactful if only you had the time and resources. Because you are about to have them.

Breaking the FID Cycle

Most people hesitate to dream of a more meaningful life for three reasons: *fear, inexperience,* and *doubt.* And when these factors get a strong emotional hold on us, they create roadblocks that work together to form a vicious cycle that stops us in our tracks.

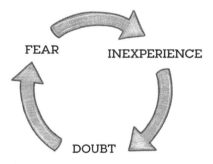

There's only one way to break free of this cycle: we have to jump in the middle of the ring and break all of them at once. Let's take a look at how our own fear, inexperience, and doubt about our financial situations keep us from moving forward with our lives.

Money and Fear

It doesn't seem like money should be so hard: spend less than you make, save for things you want, repeat. Unfortunately, it never seems to work out that way. Money fears cause stress every single day. They are relentless. Fear takes up residence in our brains like an unwanted house guest, refusing to leave even after we forget why it arrived in the first place.

The what-if worriers have it the worst. Though true financial disasters are unlikely, the consequences are significant: things like losing your job, losing your home, not being able to afford special events, incurring a big expense that you can't pay for, or never being able to stop working. Even the highest achievers I work with find money intimidating and stressful.

Here are a few things you may have been telling yourself to avoid taking charge of your finances:

- My money isn't organized enough to even look at.
- What's the point? My income and expenses are what they are.
- I'm no good with money, and I never will be.
- Why would I meet with someone just to hear them tell me to spend less and make more?
- How will doing anything for tomorrow make my life better today?

Fear is the hardest barrier to recognize because we disguise it as so many different, logical things that stop us in our tracks. We can call our lack of action practicality, intelligence, patience, or any other word that makes the problem not about us, but it's really our own fear working against us.

This book will show you a system that gives you the confidence to effectively manage your money yourself. Taking these steps helps to erase fear. Once you see the progress you can generate in a matter of days, your fears around money will slowly begin to melt away, and you'll be one step closer to breaking free of the FID cycle and planning your year off.

Money and Inexperience

Ultimately, fear boils down to avoiding the unknown, and the only cure is knowledge. To get rid of fear around money, you therefore

EXERCISE:
Face Your Money Fears

If your heart rate is rising just thinking about taking control of your money, channel that energy and list every one of your fears, right now, no matter how horrifying or unlikely.

1. ....
2. ....
3. ....
4. ....
5. ....
6. ....
7. ....
8. ....
9. ....
10. ....

This list might seem scary, but by putting a name to your fears, you'll be one step closer to conquering them.

need to create certainty and familiarity about money. Of course, that's easier said than done.

Suppose you read a ton of articles like "The Seven Best Ways to Save for Retirement." If knowledge is power, all that reading must be giving you tons of power. But does it? Not much, no. That's because the power comes through implementing that knowledge to make consistent changes in the real world. Information becomes knowledge when you *use* the information and *experience* it.

Why do so few of us understand how money works? I've noticed three primary factors that contribute to this widespread issue:

1. Financial education in the United States is minimal at best and a joke at worst. Like me, you probably learned about amoebas and argon in high school, but not about APRs and saving for the future (hence you reading random articles about retirement). When most people get their first mortgage, they don't even know what makes a loan a good choice or a risky one!

2. Parents do not prioritize teaching their children about money. But it's not their fault: if no one taught them, they didn't really *have* a system to teach you. Then, just like them, you were thrown to the wolves to figure it out for yourself.

3. Online financial literacy resources are suspect. Educating yourself online is fine if you want to learn to write computer code, but the number of clickbait headlines for finance articles that lead to poor or misleading content is scary. You won't find a good financial education online; you will find articles designed to sell you things you don't need.

Without even the most basic of answers to our mounting money questions, the lack of knowledge and experience remains, and the cycle continues. But you don't need a master's degree in finance to take control and get ahead. You just need to follow the system I will show you in this book.

However, this system will only help you if you take the steps and test it out. Set it up and run it. Play with it. Tweak it to fit you. But complete the exercises and follow the steps. In this way, information becomes knowledge, and you break the second part of the FID cycle.

EXERCISE:
Address Your Money Inexperience

It's only natural to fear what we don't understand. Now that you know all the places where money literacy and knowledge might clear up some of your concerns, list all the things you wish you knew about money.

1. ....

2. ....

3. ....

4. ....

5. ....

6. ....

7. ....

8. ....

9. ....

10. ....

Now that you know what you don't know, you can find out! And if you're not sure where to turn, the next exercise will help you figure out where to find the answers you seek.

Money and Trust

All the knowledge in the world is useless if you don't know whom to trust. Why is it so difficult to find someone who can help? After all, there are countless resources: money advice books, blogs, podcasts, radio shows, and videos galore, from celebrity money gurus to the cable network talking heads. And then there are licensed professionals: financial advisors, planners, consultants, agents, brokers, registered representatives, and analysts—oh my! They are everywhere, with every strategy, ready for a free (!) phone consultation or coffee shop meeting at any hour of the day or night.

I wonder, though: If financial gurus have mastered every topic, why isn't everyone enjoying financial success? Shouldn't one of the country's more than 200,000 financial advisors be able to solve your most pressing needs? Not necessarily. In my experience, these "advisors" spend most of their time either regurgitating the same stale advice you can get anywhere or making claims about their abilities they can't back up.

When those advisors don't work for us, we turn to the network of people we value: our family, our friends, and friends of friends. They seem wise and trustworthy, but remember the thing about nobody learning about money in school or at home? To break the final chain in the FID cycle, you need a solid, trustworthy resource that you can rely on.

What's in Your Toolbox to Give?

One great place to start looking for ways to fill this important time lies at this intersection of your experiences, skills, and interests. Here is where you are going to find that one kind of answer that helps you wake up every morning crystal-clear about why you are on

EXERCISE:
Decide Who to Trust

When we don't know where to turn, we can end up over-whelmed and floundering. List all the people, resources, and institutions you know you can turn to for good advice.

1. ....

2. ....

3. ....

4. ....

5. ....

6. ....

7. ....

8. ....

9. ....

10. ....

If you're stumped for answers, here's one excellent place to start: this book. Don't listen to me because I think I have all the answers; listen to me because I have actually helped other people do this. I have no investments or insurance policies to sell you. Most importantly, I know it works, because I've implemented the Year Off Money System in my own life, for my own family.

this planet. In this section, we are going to take a quick inventory of the tools you have in your toolbox *right now* that you might consider using during your break. Later, we will consider what you want to get out of your year, both personally and professionally. Then, by completing the exercises and working through the simple money strategies throughout the rest of the book, you will have all the tools you need for a successful year off. Finally, you will create a list of activities to try, organizations to meet with, and areas of interest to explore.

I believe you have been made the way you are for a reason, and that reason is to find your own individual way to help other people. Whether you believe that or not, I hope you agree that there is something unique about you, including the ways you can contribute and make a difference for others. It's likely your path to greater purpose resides at the center of what makes you *you*. For example, your *experiences* have allowed you to see things now in ways that you couldn't before. The *skills* you have acquired along the way give you the tools to get the job done. Your *interests* reflect your personality and provide motivation to keep going, even when things aren't going as planned.

Let's take a look at each of these aspects to see what you could offer the world.

Your Experiences

All that you have experienced in your life makes you different from everyone else on the planet. Nobody breathing the same air has gone through what you have, for better and for worse. Your siblings, best friends, and coworkers may have shared many defining moments with you, but the collection of everything you have seen makes you unique.

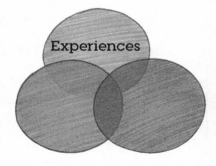

Additionally, your experiences and how you handled them have brought you perspective, lessons, and personal insights that can be valuable to others. And I'm not necessarily talking about your work experience. Everything is on the table here. Maybe your childhood was difficult, you struggled with your health, or you were attacked by a gang of clowns as an adult. Working through any of these incidents will provide you with wisdom and real-world experience that you can pass on to others who may be struggling in similar situations.

If you have wrestled with addiction recovery, for instance, you may find it meaningful to help others who are still fighting that battle. If you spent time in the military, you understand what discipline (or a lack thereof) can do to a person. Those with management or sales experience may be able to bring all they have mastered to a struggling nonprofit that has never provided accountability for its employees.

A friend of mine who is a recovering alcoholic found himself owning several different recovery houses, places where men live together and get support while they try to break free from their addictions. My friend did not go searching for this opportunity; someone found him once he started sharing his life experience with others. Painful events from the past don't have to stay buried. You can bring them up to the surface to help others avoid a similar fate.

Your memories likely cover the whole spectrum of human emotion, and there is no telling which ones you can draw on in the future to help others. If you are like me, it may be easiest to remember the painful experiences, but think of your positive experiences as well.

When I listed out the experiences that shaped my life prior to my year off, I was surprised to see how much leadership experience I had. From college through present day, I have continuously been involved in helping some type of organization achieve its mission. When I looked more closely, I realized that at each place, I had become involved in leadership almost instantly. This surprised me, until I realized that I have owned my own business for most of my

27

EXERCISE:
Consider Your Experiences

What comes to mind when you think about your own life experiences? Imagine that you are contacted by a Hollywood screenwriter who wants to write the story of your life. To make a compelling movie, she wants to know four or five life experiences that defined you. What were the ups and downs in your life that changed how you viewed the world? Write them down in the following list.

1. ....

2. ....

3. ....

4. ....

5. ....

6. ....

7. ....

8. ....

9. ....

10. ....

You may not be able to recall and rank your most significant experiences on demand, and that's okay. Keep thinking about it. Important memories and noteworthy events have a funny way of popping into your mind when you least expect them. Return to this list over the next several weeks, and keep it updated as you think of new experiences.

life and have been managing employees for over fifteen years. It made sense. What have you spent most of your life doing? You might have far more experience than you realize.

Your Skills

Have you ever taken a moment to catalog and truly appreciate the breadth of skills you have acquired during your lifetime? You have likely become magnificent at a wide variety of things in your life, though they may seem minor to you. If you want to get serious about making an impact in this world, a sober analysis of what skills you picked up throughout your life is a necessity. Let's do it.

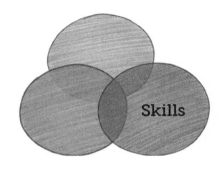

First, let's make sure we're not limiting ourselves to only our concrete, tangible skills. Skills can be divided into two major types— hard and soft—and every day, we all draw from both skill sets.

Hard Skills

Hard skills are easy to demonstrate to others. They are often learned and practiced and can include writing, computer programming, operating machinery, speaking a foreign language, or painting houses. For example, my hard skills include creating spreadsheets, developing websites, parallel parking, and sitting in the hot tub for extended periods of time.

Yours may be completely different. Don't stress out if your list doesn't include singing, walking tightropes, kickboxing, or anything else you have convinced yourself is cool over the years. Your primary hard skill can be accurate data entry, and with the right system, you can add more value to society than any wannabe singer this world has produced. Just be honest here—no judgments.

Soft Skills

Soft skills are a little trickier to identify, but they're arguably more important in the grand scheme of things. While hard skills may grab the headlines (e.g., sick dance moves), it takes a different list of skills to move forward in a world where everyone has their own agenda. These capabilities can include patience, leadership, problem-solving, teamwork, motivating others, cheerfulness, or any other hard-to-define attribute you can think of. Soft skills are what hold teams together and move large projects forward.

For example, my soft skills are patience, problem-solving, risk-taking, making people laugh (possibly a delusion), and hiring good editors for writing projects beyond my skill level. Yours may include punctuality, telling inappropriate jokes, accepting criticism, and apologizing (possibly in that order). Your soft skills are unique to *you*. They are what you bring to every project and every purpose larger than yourself.

Your Interests

How interesting is your job? Chances are it was at least *slightly* interesting to you at some point, even if it lacks excitement now. Not all of us can work for the CIA, research cures for cancer, or understudy a champion matador. Whether or not your job is boring, your year off should allow you to explore a path you are truly interested in or walk one that you deeply enjoy. And who knows, this time may lead you to look for a new line of work or side opportunities to keep more meaning in your life.

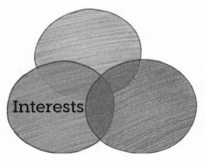

EXERCISE:
Consider Your Skills

Listing all the things we're good at can feel awkward. Listing our experiences is easy; those are just facts. No bragging is involved. Our skills, however, can feel like a matter of opinion—usually other people's—rather than the cold, hard truth of who we are. Accepting your brilliance can be especially challenging if you possess a skill that comes particularly easily, especially for self-critical types like me. Some people were born to dance, some were built to do math. Those who have seen me close down a Halloween party to "The Humpty Dance" can attest to my math skills.

But to better serve others and find our true purpose in this world—during our year off and beyond—we have to be honest with ourselves about all we have to offer.

If you are still unclear about your skills, ask those around you. Feed a couple of drinks to your significant other, and I promise you will get an honest evaluation of your skills. (You may have to be patient while they relay the list of things you are completely incapable of, but eventually, a few nuggets will point you in the right direction.)

Imagine that Armageddon is about to wipe the planet of all living beings. Your application for a secret hideout bunker includes listing the skills you can bring to the new world. (This is actually the plot to *Deep Impact*, not *Armageddon*, but you know what I mean.) What makes you useful and unique in the broadest sense?

(continue)

EXERCISE:
Consider Your Skills (cont.)

List all your hard and soft skills below.

Hard Skills   Soft Skills

1. ....

2. ....

3. ....

4. ....

5. ....

6. ....

7. ....

8. ....

9. ....

10. ....

For me, after creating personal financial plans for nearly twenty years, it would be a stretch to say I find the process as fascinating as I did ten years ago. But I acknowledge my skills and experience in this area. I see the value to others in how I spend my days, and I don't need to leave the only profession I have ever known just because I'm having a midlife crisis.

For my year, however, I wanted to explore new, engaging areas of life while tapping my financial skills and experience. To do this, I created a podcast (finance with a *large* dose of humor), books, and online courses to help those who struggle with money. I didn't need to abandon my profession because I was bored; I simply needed to supplement my day with activities that I found much more interesting, like writing and podcasting.

Your interests—especially those you rarely have time for or have never let yourself explore—can play a big part in how you want to spend your year off. Perhaps you have always wanted to learn a language, play an instrument, or master a specific technology. Maybe you simply want to share what you already know with the world. Regardless, if your new pursuit is more interesting than how you are currently spending your day, then why hold back?

EXERCISE:
Consider Your Interests

Think about the last time you were sitting on the couch, phone in hand, scrolling through your social media feed, when something truly interesting caught your eye and you said to yourself, "Wow, I always wanted to do that." It may seem like vacations, youth sports, and politics are the only things that ever pop up in your social media feed, but I assure you there are more. Dig deeper. What grabs your attention on a regular basis? What do you see other people doing that you wish you could do? What if time and money weren't problems?

Think about the last time a total stranger told you what they did for a living, and you answered "that's amazing" and meant it. What did that person do? Why did you respond that way? Your interest could have been piqued by traveling, speaking to groups, playing with new technology, or working with a specific group of people.

(continue)

33

EXERCISE:
Consider Your Interests (cont.)

Take a moment to think about the last several times your curiosity was piqued by someone else's job. Don't hold back–the sky's the limit. Whatever comes to mind, list it here.

1. ....

2. ....

3. ....

4. ....

5. ....

6. ....

7. ....

8. ....

9. ....

10. ....

This list may feel like an inventory of your past hopes and secret dreams, but it's becoming something much more concrete: a road map for your future. Where you've been, what you've seen, what you are able to accomplish, and what interests or inspires you–these factors form the foundation for what you can do on your year off to enjoy your life while making a difference in the world.

The Sweet Spot

Now that you've taken a clear look at everything you have to offer, let's look at ways to leverage what you've come up with for a more rewarding break from your regular life.

Look for the Overlap

The goal of these exercises is to find the place where your experience, skills, and interests overlap with each other. Finding an opportunity to pursue that integrates a few areas of your life is truly an "aha" moment. You may feel you are discovering something that has been waiting for you the whole time.

This next exercise didn't give me the answer right away either, but it did give me a way to start thinking. Rather than be cornered into something finance-related, I realized my experience includes developing and implementing new projects quickly. The majority of my skills have a technical bent (finance, accounting, technology, etc.), but one of my soft skills that I enjoy is educating others, which I have been doing as a financial planner for most of this century.

Sounds great, but does any of that *interest* me? Not really; what interests me is writing. I have always wanted to communicate thoughts and ideas to others in the same clear, succinct manner that so many great writers do. And to do that from my own house (pants optional) is an introvert's dream come true!

So, if we take a fearlessness in launching new projects, the skills to educate others about topics I have experienced, and a love of writing, what do we get? This book! With the time off that I carved out from my primary job, I wrote the book you're reading now in order to help others achieve the same amazing experience I was able to achieve.

Is this my true purpose in life? I don't know, but it is inarguably a great place to start. I can't fast-forward to the end and see what the most important thing in my life was; all I can do is get started now. I encourage you to do the same.

Don't Rule Anything Out

When I started searching for more purpose in my life, I caught myself immediately ruling ideas out before I even started. I remember thinking, "I want to use my skills and talents to help as many people as possible. I don't want to stand in a soup line serving food to one person at a time!" My next thought was, "Wait—have I ever actually stood in a soup line serving meals to the homeless?" Not since I was about twelve. It's not that I am above working with the homeless. I just figured that my substantial business experience would lead to something more . . . leveraged.

If you aren't sure whether you will like something, try it before you rule it out, no matter how crazy or unlikely it sounds. For example, my wife used to put ketchup on her tacos. At some point she did something totally irrational, tried it, and discovered that she liked it. (I'm still trying to get her into counseling.)

Here's another example. If you currently work as a Registered Nurse, don't feel that your only option is to give malaria shots to kids in Africa (although that would be cool). You may have totally different skills, like playing the piano. Your first instinct, when evaluating your skills, may be to list the hard skills like taking temperatures, starting IVs, giving shots, and other sciencey things that finance geeks like me don't understand. It is highly likely, however, that you have also picked up valuable communication (soft) skills that enable you to translate complex information into everyday words or work easily with people who are emotional. If this is your combination of experience, skills, and interests, and if your heart sings when you think of helping victims of abuse find joy by playing the piano, it is certainly worth a try. Why not give a few lessons?

The key here is to *give your idea a shot.* Keep moving. Explore. Only by getting in the car and driving somewhere can you determine whether you are happy with your destination.

What Do You Want to Experience?

Somewhere along the line, between bills, babies, and back pain, we all become less intentional about how we spend our time. Fires need to be put out, problems solved, and money earned to pay for it all. But trying (and too often failing) to squeeze the things you care about into your schedule is no way to live.

Wandering aimlessly through your time off of work won't help you find meaning and purpose any more than wandering aimlessly through a career you dislike. Without a schedule and plan for your activities, brushing your teeth in the morning becomes your biggest accomplishment of the day. It's never too late to look for deeper meaning in your life, and your year off is a great time to change direction. This is your opportunity to flip life's priorities—to intentionally schedule the most important people and activities into your life first, then fit everything else around what you have chosen to focus on.

Now that you have a sense of the tools you can use during your year off, the next big factor to consider is: What are your goals? What do you want to get out of this time? What do you want to experience or contribute to this world?

Let's consider a few categories of activities to start moving in the right direction.

Service

Focusing time and energy on yourself is a hollow exercise if the end result doesn't benefit anyone else. We are after meaning here, not establishing new personal records for your existing hobbies. The obvious solution to add meaning to your life is to spend more time helping other people.

EXERCISE:
Put It All Together

Now that you have written out your own experiences, skills, and interests, copy them all onto one page, and look at what might come out of the space in the middle. (Use a separate sheet if you need more room.) Ask friends and family to help you brainstorm. What do you have in your toolbox? What could you build with it?

Get creative! Picture that you have been asked to speak at the National Airing-of-Grievances Conference, a three-day event held in northern Canada that has been sold out for months. You are told that people here struggle with every kind of issue you can imagine, and you're invited to choose four or five areas of your life where you have struggled and where you think your experience would most help others. Write them down below.

Experiences

....

....

....

Skills   Interests

....

....

....

....

Delivering value to others may be something you can do on your own, or you may ultimately align yourself with an existing volunteer group to help important causes in your country or overseas.

And don't feel like you have to fit within the existing volunteer structures (though it may take you some time to push past them at first). Let's say you are a sales manager who has worked in corporate America for twenty years, and you are inspired by the idea of curing diseases in developing countries. You don't necessarily have to apply for a management position in a large nonprofit to find your purpose. With your experience giving scintillating presentations about widgets or soap or whatever it is you do, your skills can translate into creating educational materials for any cause that you care about. You could contact a small organization and offer to build a workshop curriculum as well as an educational slideshow for its sad, run-down website.

A word of advice, however, for if or when you decide to approach nonprofit organizations and offer assistance in your specific area of expertise: be prepared for the volunteer coordinators you will speak with to have no idea what to do with you. They will generally be nice people who are thrilled to see you, but they will have no clue what your real talents and skills are, and they will herd you into some type of volunteer orientation, if they herd you anywhere at all. (Nonprofits are not always well-oiled machines of efficiency.) But don't let that depress you.

Even if you can't always jump in immediately, you can start by identifying your favorite nonprofit, meeting other volunteers, and looking for posted opportunities to help. Keep your eyes open for nonprofit events that look interesting and go check them out. You can introduce yourself to members of the organization, ask a few questions, and get to know the lay of the land in that organization without committing to anything yet.

Self-Improvement

Being productive isn't always easy. There are so many things we would rather be pursuing during the day, but we aren't always able to. Chances are, you have developed a routine over time to get up at a reasonable hour, get to work on time, and stay focused enough throughout the day to keep the paychecks coming.

Taking time away from your job will break you out of your current routine and force you to develop a new one. And while getting out of your rut is the whole point here, this freedom will also bring a new set of challenges.

If you sleep in until 10 a.m. on Saturdays, for instance, chances are you will start doing it on the weekdays as well. If you have a hard time not snacking when you are around the house, being around the house a lot more is just setting yourself up for a year off from your pants fitting.

Most of the problems you will run into are predictable, which means you can start solving them now. You may need to develop new habits to stay focused, or you may need to break existing habits that you know will slow you down.

Either way, it's time to take an honest look at what could potentially trip you up as you commit to new experiences. We will take a closer look at three habits you will need in Chapter 6, but start thinking about a few areas you can address *now*. Self-improvement doesn't need to wait until you have money in the bank; you can start that journey now for free.

Improved Relationships

Hands down, the number-one regret people have on their deathbeds is that they didn't spend enough time with people or pay enough attention to their relationships. How you feel about your life day to day is directly related to how healthy the relationships are that make up your life. This begins with the connection you have to your significant other, family, and children but also includes your relationships with colleagues, others at your job, and strangers you interact with. It even includes your relationship with yourself.

If all of your relationships are operating at 100 percent, then you may want to focus your time in other ways. (Congratulations on mastering life!) It is far more likely, however, that things are not entirely perfect with all your connections and that some of them could use a little more attention before you breathe your last. How valuable would you feel if you used at least some of your time off to improve existing relationships and develop new ones?

Here are four questions to consider as you make your plan:

1. Which relationships could use some repair?

If you have an estranged sibling or a great friend that you lost touch with years ago, or even if you were a jerk to the barista at your favorite coffee shop the other day, it's time to clean up that relationship. It doesn't matter who was right or wrong (although obviously you were right and everybody knows it). Your cold shoulder doesn't make you as badass as you think it does, so just reach out and move on. In your last breath, you will want to have repaired the family stuff, so put your hat in your hand and start working on your apology letter.

2. Which relationships do you want to build on?

We all have people in our lives who deserve more time and attention. Your list might include your children and your parents, but it often runs much deeper. Maybe these relationships aren't in trouble, but your connection with these important people isn't quite what you want it to be. How would you like your relationships to be? What can you do to take one small step in that direction?

3. What relationships do you want to create?

Have you been wishing you had a mentor in a new area of your life? Perhaps your coworker is a workout nut, and you've been trying to hit the gym more often. Or your neighbor doesn't drink, and you want to add nondrinking activities into your life. Or your old high school friend lives well below her means, and you'd like to cultivate those habits for yourself. We could all use more positive influences in our lives, but often we fail to add them to our circles because it puts pressure on us to improve ourselves. Now is your chance. What do you want to build?

4. What relationships drag you down that can be eliminated?

You know the old saying that you become the average of the five people you hang out with the most? There is some truth to that, but only a self-important jerk would run around cutting close friends out of their life intentionally. Instead, let everybody you hang out with know what you are trying to become (and let your mouth-breather friends show themselves the door). If you do have truly soul-sucking or negative people in your life, it may be time to identify them and cut those folks off so they can stop dragging you down. Start now to improve your year off!

More Education

Have you been longing to further your education? Perhaps your street smarts have taken you as far as you can go in your career, and you are looking at buying a ridiculously expensive piece of paper (a.k.a., a diploma) to break through the glass ceiling. Maybe you have realized that a bachelor's degree isn't enough to keep climbing the corporate ladder and you are considering an advanced degree or some kind of certification. Perhaps you realized that you chose a career field as exciting as watching grass grow and need an education to switch tracks to something more stimulating.

If you are confident that a formal education will enhance your life, by all means, prep for your time off by checking out schools and programs and all they have to offer. Just be careful. I can't tell you how many friends of mine have gone back to school as adults to earn their MBAs only to later find out that nothing they learned actually helped them in their jobs. The only skill I picked up during college is how to take tests while hungover (sadly, a skill that still comes in handy).

With the daily introduction of more online education courses, certificates, and training programs, the days of colleges having a monopoly on adult education are dwindling. If you want to test the waters in a new occupation or wish to develop a skill you have always wanted, then you can skip the formal education and try job shadowing, information-gathering interviews, online courses or other informal training methods.

Start looking into programs now and you may discover a way to learn something useful. Or, just for fun, try your hand at cartooning, painting, bartending, or auto mechanics and come out of your year off a richer person.

A New Career

Are you interested in a taking time off work because you're dissatisfied with your job or current routine? If so, your first instinct might be to leave your career in the rearview mirror, possibly even flipping it the bird as you speed away. Don't be too certain that this action will solve the problem.

Your choice of occupation may very well be unhealthy for you, or you might just need a break, a new company, or a different boss. The point is, *you won't know for sure until you have the freedom to leave it.* Once you have the resources to do something else for a while, the answer will become crystal clear to you. Let this big decision percolate while you explore your options for your time away from your job, and don't burn any bridges you don't have to.

Perhaps the ultimate answer will involve a new line of work or even starting your own business. If you have never been an entrepreneur before but feel called to hang out your own shingle, you'll want to spend scads of time talking with experienced business owners. The reality of running your own show isn't always as glamorous as what you're picturing, so do your research extensively, and avoid getting caught up by people trying to sell you instant entrepreneurial success in a neat and expensive package.

If you do know you want to change careers, your year off *is* your chance to explore your new field. Typically, you have pressure to find a new job in a matter of months, if not weeks, which often limits your options to whatever is available at that time. Imagine the job selection possibilities with a full year to search for a new career! As long as you are organized and focused using the steps laid out in this book, twelve months is plenty of time to pursue the career you have always wanted.

EXERCISE:
Find Your Purpose

We've covered a lot of ground, and by now I'm sure your brain is swirling with new ideas for how to spend your year of freedom. That's good! Pour all your ideas out in one long rush—every last one of them—and don't stop until you're dry.

Think about the changes you want to make in your community, the relationships you want to cultivate, and the personal and professional goals you want to set for yourself. How do those hopes and dreams intersect the experiences, skills, and interests you listed above? Write down everything you'd like to accomplish—for the world, your relationships, and yourself.

1. ....

2. ....

3. ....

4. ....

5. ....

6. ....

7. ....

8. ....

9. ....

10. ....

(continue)

EXERCISE:
Find Your Purpose (cont.)

Now, take a look at your list. (Don't worry—penmanship doesn't count.) What patterns are evident that you were expecting to see? What pictures emerge that surprise you?

You don't have to decide everything right now; feel free to return to this list whenever new ideas or inspiration strike. For now, refer back to this list and the other exercises in this chapter whenever you want, and continue to dream of all the things you'd do if only you had the time. Because you're about to *make* time.

What Do You Need to Stay on Track?

Now that you are excited about exploring the possibilities for your year off, the very next thing to do is take action! It may be tempting to dive into the next chapter and keep reading, but before you do, here are a few tips to keep you moving forward (and sane) while you count down.

Tell Others About Your Plans

Sometimes, telling the people closest to us is the hardest part. You might be afraid that if you casually mention, "Oh, by the way, I am taking a year off from work starting next week," they might think you are insane.

But it doesn't matter, because you're really going to do this. Don't keep your intentions to move your life forward a secret; start talking to people now about the ideas percolating in your mind. Let your friends and family know what you're doing and how they can help. You will be surprised how many people want to help others figure out their lives. Share with both strangers and those who are already close to you how they can be part of what you want to accomplish with your life. (And if they want to take their own long-term break from the routine, send them a copy of this book!)

Letting your friends and family know you're looking for new career or volunteer experiences doesn't just build a support system; it could open doors you didn't even know existed. Those around you may be involved with people and projects that you knew nothing about but would find fascinating, and it only takes one person to connect you to an important new contact or opportunity. And don't wait: once you let others know you are looking for ways to help, it could be at least six months before somebody sends a good idea your way, so get started!

Spending some time volunteering is always a good idea, but if you are looking for a complete career change, you can also start looking for part-time work in that new field. This may be difficult if you already work full time, but it's not impossible to find something that works for your schedule.

(Speaking of working, it may be wise to ensure that your future awesomeness is not a primary topic of conversation around the water cooler at work. Everyone there will find out in due time, but if Nina in Corporate Accounts Payable tells your boss about your plans before you do, your time off may start a bit sooner than expected. In a later chapter, we will discuss how to tell the boss and your coworkers, so hold off on that for now.)

Reach out to friends and strangers alike. They may not join you on your adventure, but you will undoubtedly see your relationship strengthen with anyone whom you let in on your plans. You may also find yourself inspiring those around you to take their own year off!

Stick to the System

While most personal finance books, worksheets, and blogs make it feel that sitting down and creating a line-by-line budget of every dollar you spend is the only responsible path to adulting, in reality, budgets are hard to come up with and even harder to stick to.

Technology was supposed to solve this problem for us. Popular online budgeting tools are intended to automate the process of tracking your spending down to the last penny. Rather than simplify our lives, however, these tools have become one more website or app you are too busy to monitor and end up not caring about.

Why doesn't it work? Life—and your spending—varies drastically each month. You don't spend $250 eating out every month, you spend $149.88 one month and $423.16 the next. You spend 50 percent more money in December and pay 20 percent more the month your car insurance bill arrives. You buy $600 of clothes one month and a pair of socks the next.

But when your budgeting system breaks and you give up, your brain files the whole thing away as a bad experience, and you swear you will never try budgeting again. From there, you manage your finances by glancing at your checking account balance every week or so. Or by whipping out plastic and figuring it out in the perpetual "later."

Although you may be paying your bills on time, when you wing it, you are not actually getting ahead. You are simply treading water while your money disappears. The hard truth is this: to leave your career for any length of time, you need a system. The process in this book is pretty simple when you take it in small bites. You just have to keep chewing.

I have learned that the key to getting closer is simple: keep moving. Imagine climbing into your vehicle in your driveway without starting the engine. Are you going to see anything cool or do anything awesome? Of course not. You can't steer a parked car! To dominate your year off, you need to keep the system running, and that means doing a little bit toward your YO System each day.

Brainstorm and Discuss With Your Accountability Partner

Here it is: your first accountability partner assignment! In Chapter 1, you identified someone who will keep you on track during your journey (and who, hopefully, is also taking their own journey). The first step is to tell them about your plans. This can feel a little intimidating, so here is an easy way to start: ask them if they have ever considered doing something different with their lives.

Use the ideas in this chapter to dig into what is working for them and what isn't. Ask what they would change if they could, who they want to spend more time with, and what activities always seem to catch their attention. Find someone to share this journey, someone you can talk to about your struggles, challenges, and accomplishments.

Set up a meeting now to discuss the ideas in this chapter, and work through your Chapter 2 accountability checklist with your partner. Then, in the next chapters, I'll show you how to prepare your money to implement the Year Off Money System for yourself.

Chapter 2 Accountability
CHECKLIST

Breaking the Cycle

1. State your number-one fear about money out loud. Inform it that you are about to punch it in the neck.

   • Complete the Face Your Money Fears exercise.

2. Brainstorm ways to get more comfortable with your money and conquer your inexperience.

   • Complete the Address Your Money Inexperience exercise.

3. Decide who you can trust to help you learn more about money.

   • Complete the Decide Who to Trust exercise.

Toolbox Inventory

4. Your Experiences

   • Complete the Consider Your Experiences exercise.

5. Your Skills

   • Complete the Consider Your Skills exercise

6. Your Interests

   • Complete the Consider Your Interests exercise.

7. The Sweet Spot

   • Complete the Put It All Together exercise.

(continue)

Chapter 2 Accountability
CHECKLIST

What You Want to Experience

8. Service
   - The first person/organization I am going to talk to about getting involved in helping others is _____.

9. Self-Improvement
   - In order to successfully manage myself, the most important habit I can strengthen or develop is _____.
   - The habit I know I will need to break is _____.

10. Improved Relationships
    - The relationship I most want to repair is with _____.
    - The relationship I most want to improve or build on is with _____.
    - The relationship I most want to create is with _____.
    - The relationship I most want to eliminate is with _____.

11. More Education
    - The knowledge I am most interested in acquiring right now is _____.

12. A New Career
    - One brand-new career that intrigues me is _____.
    - Complete the Find Your Purpose exercise.

Accountability Partner

13. Tell your AP about your progress!

CHAPTER 3

Bucketing, not Budgeting

My client's five-gallon purse teetered on the chair next to her as she rummaged through it, and I cringed. During the meeting, she had been hinting that she wanted to share something about her finances with me, but she hadn't worked up the courage yet. Were those my walking papers she was about pull out of there?

To my surprise, she retrieved something much, much worse. With a look of exasperation, she dramatically dropped about fifteen envelopes full of cash on the table. "That's our budgeting system!" she almost shouted.

This was my first sit-down with this nice lady and her husband, who explained that they were using cash to try to figure out what they were spending their money on. Every month, even with two six-figure incomes, they couldn't keep more than a thousand dollars in their checking account, and their credit card balances were steadily rising.

They had tried every system they could find to get their money under control: online software, spreadsheets, a physical journal, and even hypnosis. But with the ease of electronic transactions, their money would inevitably go to what was most urgent rather than what was most important. Finally, they had moved on to the dreaded envelopes of cash . . . but five weeks in, they were already tired of the new system.

"Let me guess," I told them, scanning the words scrawled on a few envelopes. "You don't spend the exact same amount of money every month on eating out, traveling, gas, and car insurance. You are constantly borrowing money from one envelope to another and then forgetting where it came from in the first place, so you still don't know where the money is going. On top of that, you don't like carrying around wads of cash, because this isn't 1982 and you aren't a drug dealer."

They looked at each other and then nodded at me. "Can you help?"

Financial trouble is the leading cause of stress in a relationship (a fact I can confirm with firsthand experience). The number of otherwise-healthy relationships lost over the years due to spats over why who bought what must be staggering. What I see in my office is that couples fight over money when they don't have the proper information and aren't on the same page. One person is arguing about a recent expense at a clothing store, and the other is frustrated at the overall lack of money in the checking account.

Instead, a plan where both partners can see the trade-offs they are making at a glance cuts down on the arguments. If we take on a car payment, what are we giving up? If we want to save for a year off, where will the money come from?

The good news is that when you do find the right system, few things are more rewarding than working with your partner or spouse to go on the offense with your spending and accomplish goals that are important to both of you. (By reading this book, you're taking one step closer to experiencing this bliss.)

This chapter will outline the YO System for you, help you understand your cash flow, and lay important groundwork for setting up your own system of managing your money. Then, in the next chapter, I will walk you through setting up this system for yourself.

The Year Off Money System

In order to take a break from your job, you must implement a simple money system to get you there and get you through it. The Year Off

Money System is designed to help you accomplish this without having to feel pressured, helpless, or frustrated when you spend your money. But make no mistake: there is no magic in these pages. Simply reading this book will not fix your money problems. Taking the steps and doing the exercises will.

If how you've been handling your finances hasn't been working, it's time to change up your strategy. (That's why you're holding this book!) Do something different with your money, and you will get different results. Better results. And best of all, you will get to find out how long until you can take a year off.

Peace in Your Household

One day, I was working with a client to help them budget when I saw their eyes start to glaze over. They did not care what a reasonable clothing budget was. The husband needed $125 a year for his Costco wardrobe and wondered why his wife's clothing budget had so many zeros. Finally, out of exasperation, they asked, "What the hell do you do, Steve? Do you and your wife have these stupid conversations?"

In that moment, I realized two things. One, my wife and I had not had a money argument in quite a while, and two, our household system was working so well that I hadn't even noticed. This system had evolved, one step at a time, over many years. I taught it to these clients (who loved it) and got inspired to figure out why it works so well.

I confess, my household doesn't budget. Yes, you heard me—the household of a CPA and Certified Financial Planner does not budget. If I were single, I probably would: just me and a spreadsheet (and whiskey and nineties rap). Of course, if I were single, I would not have eaten a vegetable in a long time either . . .

Over the first few years of my marriage, I created no fewer than twenty spreadsheets and set up our finances on multiple pieces of software. None of it worked for us. Our attitudes toward money and spending were too different. I thought we should exclusively buy secondhand (and often third- or fourth-hand) furniture so we could start saving money. She thought we needed more throw pillows in our life and made weekly visits to Target to fill our couch and bed with them.

We had to find a common money language to speak that didn't center around the daily transactions in our checking account. It took time, but we did it.

If you are part of a household, the challenge of managing your finances becomes more complex. (Single people, bear with me for a moment.) Not only do you have extra income and expenses to track, you also have the biggest challenge of all: finding a way to discuss finances without arguing. And everyone has a different relationship with money. What works for one person rarely works for another. That means finding a finance style for two people is not twice as hard—it is a hundred times as hard.

To place less stress on your relationship, you need a system that shows you where your money is coming in and going out so that you can spend intentionally. Ideally, this system also controls where you want it to go.

If you have tried your best to budget and didn't make it past a month or two, you are not alone. Most people are not bean counters, and, too often, budgeting simply does not work. You simply need a money system that allows couples to get on the same financial page. You need a common framework for discussing personal finances instead of trying to speak in the foreign language of numbers.

If budgeting on a spreadsheet or in software works for you, keep doing it. The best system is always one that you will stick to. If you use a category or envelope system to withdraw the cash you need each month, and if this system is up and running successfully, congratulations—keep going.

If whatever you are using is not working and is causing undue stress on your relationships, however, let it go and use this system instead. Paying continuous attention to details you don't care about is a poor long-term plan.

Money Isn't the Problem

Isn't it odd? We each have different education, experiences, and work ethics, yet we all seem to make the exact same amount of money: not enough.

You likely make more money than you ever have, but is your life more meaningful and joyous? Do you have anything substantial to show for all that additional income? The answer for most everyone is "no." The more that comes in, the more that goes out. Life is different, but not necessarily better.

We are going to change this. Right now.

First, recognize that having a rising income that doesn't improve your life doesn't make you bad with money. It makes you human. What makes you *good* with money is that you are about to implement a system to help hang on to more of your money and put it to good use.

When we don't understand how money works, it's easy to call undesirable financial results a "money problem." But is it really? "Money problem" is a catchall category for any specific issues that are blocking you from going where you want to go. What makes a money problem a problem is that you can't see it. You can't get a sense of where the money is going.

Perhaps you have too many bills for your income, but the bills arrive irregularly, and you can't see the trend. Your monthly overhead costs could simply be too high to make any progress. Maybe your bills are under control, but you spend too much on entertainment, living like Beyoncé, except nobody comps your meals and drinks. (You are only a couple million Instagram followers away, though.) It's even possible that you spend like a reasonable human being and simply earn less than you need. Sometimes, making more money really is the solution, and we shouldn't overcomplicate things.

Whatever your situation, the first step is simple: let's figure out where you are today. I'm not telling you to quit buying shoes, sell your boat, or stop living your life. For now, we are simply going to look at where your money is going. If this makes you nervous . . . good. That means it's worth doing. (Just don't let it scare you into skipping the rest of this chapter.)

If you can see it, you can fix it—and that's what the YO System is all about. It's time to group together the different pieces of your financial life so you can see what is going on.

Your Income Bucket

Let's start with an easy one: How much money do you actually make? How much comes in? This total inflow of cash is your Income Bucket.

Predictable Money

Step one is to get a handle on the regular, consistent income that you make each month. This includes all the money in your bank account that you can rely on being there.

Predictable money is typically generated from your primary job but can come from many places:

- Your job(s)
- Your spouse's job(s)
- Rental income
- Commissions, royalties, or other payouts
- Consistent investment income
- Alimony
- Child support
- Government payments, disability, or pensions
- Trust fund income
- Other

Remember, "predictable" is the key here. Even if your sports betting skills are getting stronger every week or you are cleaning up by selling hand-me-downs in the virtual garage sale, that isn't regular income. For now, we're just counting the stuff you know you can count on.

Gross or Net?

You may feel like all of your paychecks are "gross" because you are criminally underpaid, but that isn't what that term means. Gross wages are what you earn before they steal—I mean *deduct*—taxes and benefits from your paycheck. Net wages are what actually lands in your bank account.

For example, say you accepted a salary of $72,000 per year. As you have no doubt noticed, you are not seeing $6,000 ($72,000/12) drop into your bank account each month. You are likely seeing around two-thirds of that amount in your account each month. The $72,000 is your *gross wage*, and—sit down—the $48,000 a year you actually receive is your *net wage*. In this exercise, you need to use your actual, or net, wage.

In recent years, employers have taken to calling your overall employment structure "total compensation." This number takes your salary and adds in some expenses your employer pays: taxes, insurance and other benefits, parking passes, and so on. Now you know how expensive you are to an organization. This number makes the employer look cool, but it does nothing to help you. You can't spend either gross wages or total compensation. The only number that matters to you is the cash deposit that hits your bank account: your net wage.

Semipredictable Money

When I teach this system, one of the biggest questions I hear is this: "How do I assign a monthly number to my income when it varies from month to month?" I'm pleased that you asked, kind stranger, because self-employed people need a reliable money system more than anyone. I've noticed that when income varies, it can create a feast-or-famine mindset. When business is slow, you try to spend less (but kind of haphazardly). And when that big check finally comes in, you have a mental list of items you have been depriving yourself of and are ready to splurge.

It turns out that the problem lies with irregular *spending*, not income. Even if this amount varies every month, you'll want to take those sources of income into account.

Small Business Income

For small business owners, the line between personal and business money is often blurry, making it difficult to know exactly how much money is coming and going. The solution to this problem is beyond the scope of this book, but suffice it to say that you need to keep your business expenses (and income) separate from your personal money if you want to be an adult.

How do you create consistent monthly spending when your income isn't consistent from month to month? For now, just take your annual income from last year's tax return and divide it by twelve to estimate your monthly income. That income may not actually show up in equal amounts each month, but it will show up, and we can work with it.

Side Hustles

If you don't have a formal business of your own but bring in some extra cash from a side hustle, that is great too! Jarring pickles on the weekends or giving trombone lessons can be great ways to bring in extra cash. Whatever it is, consider this money part of your income.

Your Overhead Bucket

Remember that time you were tight on money, called your mortgage company or landlord, and calmly explained that you weren't going to be able to make your payment that month, and they told you not to worry about it?

Neither do I.

Our bills don't care what is going on in our life. Whether we get a raise at work or lose our job, the bills keep on coming. Businesses call bills that repeat "overhead expenses" (perhaps because we all have a tendency to get in *over our heads* and take on more expenses than we can handle). In this section, we look at these "necessary" expenses we can't easily get out of.

EXERCISE:
Consider Your Income Bucket

What's in your "in" bucket? Believe it or not, I find that most people are off by 20 percent or more when they estimate their income. That's not a mistake you can afford to make.

Take a reality check. Scroll through your online banking and look at the money that has been deposited into your bank accounts in the past twelve months. Write down all consistent, predictable, cash deposits as a monthly income number. If you have to divide your annual income by 12, do that.

Income Example		Your Income
Spouse 1 Wages:	$6,200	....
Spouse 2 SE Income:	$2,800	....
Rental Income:	$600	....
Side Hustle:	$250	....
Total:	$9,850	....

Your second bucket of money is an *out* bucket. Because everything else in the YO System flows from this overhead bucket, it's crucial to take a careful inventory of all your overhead expenses and find out exactly what's going into it.

What to Do If You're Irregular

Like your payroll deposits, your mortgage, internet, and cell phone bills arrive on schedule every month, in similar amounts. Pairing your monthly bills with your monthly income rarely harms a well-crafted spending plan. But when big bills show up quarterly or annually, the interruption presents a whole different problem. You may pay your car insurance annually or your life insurance quarterly. And what about Christmas or holidays? Can anything blow up a spending system faster than Old Saint Nick, the patron saint of consumer debt? If you are one of those families that spends two or three grand on Christmas every year [author shifts uncomfortably in his chair], that is a real expense that needs to be accounted for.

For now, we are simply getting a handle on all of your expenses. Take your holiday spending, divide the number by twelve, and add it to your monthly overhead bucket.

Do the same with your auto insurance and any other infrequent but recurring expenses. Turn each big bill into a monthly dollar amount so you can see what is really going on in your financial life.

Your "Future You" Buckets

So far in this chapter, you have gained clarity on exactly how much income you have to fund your life and what kind of monthly overhead you have committed yourself to. What comes next? Let's talk about the future.

We are taught that saving money is very good and spending it is less good. This is true, except that it misses one important distinction: even your "savings" will be spent some day. The reality is that you are not quite building a *savings* account; you are building a *future spending* account.

Saving money is difficult because thinking about spending money on our vague future selves is far less satisfying than actually spending money on our current selves. Why take two undefined vacations in the future when you can have one right now? Beaches are warm and drinks are cold today; who knows about the future?

Let's say your adult life will run from age twenty-two to age ninety-two. (Calling myself an adult at thirty-two would have been a stretch, let alone at twenty-two, but just go with me here.) You

EXERCISE:
Calculate Your Overhead Bucket

The best way to identify your expenses is to list every monthly, quarterly, or annual bill that you are currently committed to that help you maintain your current standard of living. Start now by listing your personal bills, expenses, debt payments—all of your obligations that aren't going away anytime soon.

Consider items such as these:

- Home expenses: mortgage or rent, property tax, home-owner's insurance and umbrella, condo fees, etc.
- Car: loan payment or lease, insurance
- Utilities: gas, electric, water, sewer
- Communications: phone, internet, cable, TV, entertainment subscriptions (Netflix, Amazon Prime, etc.)
- Maintenance: home, yard, car, toys
- Gym membership
- Other debt payments
- Irregular expenses (see previous section)

You may be making other payments that aren't traditionally considered "bills." Examples of these are alimony, child support payments, a debt you are paying back to a family member, or your membership in the jelly-of-the-month club. Whatever it is, if it's a regular expense, write it down.

(continue)

EXERCISE:
Calculate Your Overhead Bucket (cont.)

Dive deep into those bank and credit card statements! Find anything that you are paying on a regular basis and add it to the list below.

Monthly Overhead Example		Your Monthly Overhead Expenses
Rent/Mortgage:	$2,200	....
Utilities:	$325	....
Internet:	$85	....
TV/Cable:	$80	....
Auto Insurance:	$185	....
Student Loan:	$230	....
Car Loan:	$410	....
Other Debt Payments:	$650	....
Gym Membership:	$85	....
Cell Phone:	$250	....
Total Overhead:	$4,500	....

This may feel like budgeting, but I promise you it isn't. It doesn't force you to track every last expense, but rather to simply monitor three basic categories of spending. Before we can get there, however, we need data. Take this one honest look at what is going on with your personal overhead, and then it's all downhill skiing from here.

can take one of two basic financial paths throughout your seventy potential years of adulthood:

1. Work for seventy years, and spend your income for seventy years as it comes in. When you are old and don't want to work anymore, your income will drop because your salary will disappear, and you will be left with a small amount of Social Security income. You will take a huge hit to your lifestyle, because you never set up a future spending account—a retirement account—to live from.

2. Work for forty years while saving, and spend equal amounts of money for the full seventy years. This strategy requires setting aside some of your money while working now to spend later. (Some call this a "retirement account," but that assumes you want to stop working entirely. It's really just a future spending account.)

So, decide: Do you want to work when you are eighty? Will you even be able to? If not, you need a future spending account. And if you want to take a year off soon to do cool things, you need a spending account specifically for that, too. It's clear we need to focus on two very different times in our lives: the short term and the long term.

"Spend Soon" Accounts

These are places you may be contributing money toward on a regular basis that would not be considered typical "retirement accounts." Examples of these "spend soon" accounts might be the following.

- Bank savings
- Money market
- Certificate of deposit (CD)
- Investment account
- Savings bonds from grandparents
- Cash hidden in the house
- Digital payment apps (PayPal, Cash App, Venmo, etc.)
- Other

If you don't have anything to list here, that's fine. But if you're squirreling money away for later, and it isn't money specifically intended for your golden years, it's important to calculate that along with the larger financial picture.

"Spend Later" Accounts

Hopefully, you are already putting money into a future spending account, so you don't have to work when you're a grumpy old person. (If you haven't started that account yet or you're not actively contributing to it, don't worry—I've got a solution for that too.)

Examples of these "spend later" accounts might be the following:

- 401(k)
- Other work retirement plan
- Roth IRA
- Traditional IRA
- Permanent life insurance
- Investment account
- Rental property

Future spending accounts give you the flexibility to accomplish your goals. The future could have many different versions of you, some much happier than others; you should prepare for all of them. If you are not in the habit of rewarding Future You, don't fret. You still have plenty of time to get started. If you are setting aside money for the future—for both versions of Future You—this is the time to make a quick list of where all of it is going.

To accomplish what is important and meaningful to you, it's critical to set aside money for the future. If you are stuck in a dead-end job or don't have some extra resources to help others when you want to, then what the hell are you even doing? The path to meaning starts with finding money every month that you aren't going to spend.

EXERCISE:
List Your Future Accounts

Make a list of every financial account you have from which you aren't spending money on a regular basis. Next to each account, determine the dollar amount you are putting into this account on a regular basis and enter it below.

For this exercise, we care about the monthly amount going in, not the total balance already there. (If you make an annual contribution, simply divide that number by twelve. If you're not currently contributing to an account, enter zero.)

Your Spend Soon Accounts
Account Name | Monthly Addition

Your Spend Later Accounts
Account Name | Monthly Addition

....	$	....	$ ....
....	$	....	$ ....
....	$	....	$ ....
....	$	....	$ ....
....	$	....	$ ....
Total:	$	**Total:**	$ ....

Keep these totals for later reference, but for now, add the two numbers together to get your total "Future Spending" number.

And if you haven't been setting aside money on a regular basis (thus shafting Future You), don't worry: this is only a snapshot of where you are today. In the upcoming chapters, you will set up your own buckets and learn how to make up for lost time in saving money.

Lifestyle Bucket

You may have noticed we didn't cover your day-to-day spending, the twenty to thirty smaller transactions you make every week to run your life. This is where, in most magic money solution books, you are supposed to decide that you want to spend $250 a month on groceries, $100 on gas, an average of $267 a month on travel, and so on.

However, with the YO System, you don't have to list out your expenses. That would be budgeting, and budgeting is unnecessary. Although you don't need to list out all your lifestyle expenses, you do need to understand them.

Your lifestyle spending is everything you buy that was not listed in the overhead bucket or your Future You buckets. Where your overhead expenses are roughly the same every month, your lifestyle spending is more volatile and will vary from month to month. This bucket splashes a bit.

Your lifestyle spending may include:

- Groceries
- Gas
- Dining out
- Entertainment
- Clothing
- Shoes
- Technology
- Household furniture
- Travel
- A new pillow from Target every week
- Gifts
- Unlimited crap for kids
- Home improvement projects

If you were let go from your job (or, say, did something crazy like take a long-term break from it), your mortgage would still need to be paid, but you wouldn't need to take that third summer vacation with the family. Your cell phone company would still want the same amount each month, but you could choose to eat out less often to save money or, even more dramatically, buy store-brand ketchup.

The key difference is that you have instant control over your lifestyle spending. You can make changes to your habits immediately. You do not have to wait for a debt to be paid off, a cell phone contract to expire, or your car or house to sell. It is because of this instant control—and the scourge of impulse purchases—that these expenses vary so wildly from month to month.

EXERCISE:
Estimate Your Lifestyle Expenses

There are only so many places your money can go, and we have already figured out most of them. Rather than dive into how much money a certain member of your household spent at TJ Maxx last month, you can figure out your lifestyle expenses with a quick cheat.

Here is how to figure out your lifestyle spending. Just plug your monthly totals from above into the following blanks:

Lifestyle Example		Your Lifestyle:
Income Bucket (less)	$10,000	....
Overhead Bucket (less)	$4,500	....
Future Spending (equals)	$500	....
Lifestyle Bucket	$5,000	....

There it is: your lifestyle spending number! Whatever you don't spend on bills or put away for the future, you are spending on your lifestyle. Calculating your lifestyle expenses in one chunk like this is much easier than going through your bank statements and trying to add up all of your transactions at Starbucks. It's just not necessary.

Your "Final" Bucket Snapshot

Congratulations—you have accurately mapped out your financial life! How does that feel? Better than you thought it would?

However it turned out, *the hard part is behind you.* It is not possible to take twelve months off until you understand where your money is going today, and you just did that. Now, we have just one calculation to complete before we can walk away with a complete snapshot of all your buckets.

EXERCISE:
Calculate Your Expense Percentages

Knowing what percent of your income each bucket absorbs makes it easier to track your money progress over time. For example, if your income is $10,000 per month and your overhead expenses are $4,500 per month, your overhead expense is 45 percent ($4,500/$10,000) of your income.

Calculate the percentages for your overhead, lifestyle, and future spending buckets here. You'll need it for the next exercise, where we'll look at the total picture.

Monthly Overhead $	Monthly Lifestyle $	Future Spending $ ....
Divided by	Divided by	Divided by
Monthly Income $	Monthly Income $	Monthly Income $ ....
=	=	=
............%	............%	............%

There is no such thing as "right" or "wrong" with your percentages today–this is only a measure of your current reality. Later, we'll focus on what your buckets should look like for you to take your year off.

EXERCISE:
Complete Your Final Bucket Snapshot

Now that we have all the pieces of your financial life calculated, let's put it all together. This chart will be your starting point. It will allow us to calculate how many months away you are from freedom.

So few people take the time to understand what percentage of their money is allocated to each area of their life. Doing so will help you accomplish your goals and give you bragging rights over your friends who are still wrestling with spreadsheets! Enter your Income Bucket total into the worksheet below. Then, fill in the other numbers.

Your Net Monthly Income

$ ....

Monthly Overhead	Monthly Lifestyle	Monthly Future
$	$	Spending $ ....
Monthly Overhead	Monthly Lifestyle	Monthly Future
%	%	Spending % ....

Move Your Money to the Right

Take a look at your three expense buckets. In my experience, spending too much money on the left side of your plan (overhead expenses) is the main cause of financial stress. Concentrating your money there creates uncertainty and anxiety—it increases your obligations and reduces your options. It corners you and limits your freedom. I know that wasn't your plan, but often this is how expenses evolve over time when you can't see them this clearly.

Before we move on and set up your own YO System, I'd like to briefly share an excellent stress-reducing money strategy you can start to implement *right now*. It's simple: Look at your final bucket snapshot from the exercise above, and think about moving as much of your money as you can to the right, *away* from overhead and *toward* future spending.

Think about what this shift means for a minute in theory, without stressing about actually doing it. Imagine being able to reduce your overhead spending and trade that in for an increase in lifestyle spending. Lifestyle spending is based on choice, but overhead is based on obligation. With this shift, you'd experience more freedom and choice in your life. How would that feel?

In Chapter 7, we'll look at powerful ways to accelerate the system I've taught you so you can move up your year off date by months or even years. For now, in preparation for the work we'll do in the next chapter, here are a few things to consider as you focus on ways to move your money to the right.

Don't Touch the Kitchen

Not long ago, clients of mine in their early forties came to my office for their annual financial review. One of them had received a raise earlier that year because their job was going so well. Naturally, I wanted to know what they did with the extra money. "We took out a home equity loan and finally finished remodeling the kitchen, then bought a sick wakeboarding boat!" they exclaimed. As excited as I was for them, I couldn't stop thinking, "You spent your raise on *more* debt payments?"

Judgment isn't part of my job (it's a bonus I provide for free), but I do feel obligated to explain the consequences of the poor financial choices I see folks make. There is nothing wrong with a nice kitchen or a cool boat, but think about what this couple did. They received a household raise, and then spent that money on permanent overhead, on things that will create more payments for the next ten years. That extra money turned into even *less* flexibility and freedom in their lives. They can't lose their jobs now, not even one of them. By adding that raise into overhead instead of spending it on their lifestyle or saving it for the future, they pushed their prospects of time off even further away.

There is no "right" or "wrong" way to spend your money. There is only allocating your money according to your goals and desires. What confused me is that this couple had told me they wanted to save money to create more career flexibility. They wanted to move their money to the right, but without realizing it, they did the opposite.

If you don't want to take a significant break from work, then buying a boat you use every weekend might make sense. If you do want time off to explore your life, then a fancy kitchen can probably wait. And you need to make that spending choice now, *before* you get the raise.

Reconsider Credit Cards

Using credit cards typically creates more problems than it solves, but they have become a standard part of our lives. Are airlines miles really worth paying a 15 percent interest rate? Not usually, especially when the only "free ticket" available is a middle seat to Billings, Montana.

Here's the thing. You can use a credit card in the YO System, but there is a catch: each card has to be used for either overhead only or for lifestyle only, but not a mix. More than one card creates more opportunity for fudging your system; pick one account to associate it with, and set it up for automatic monthly payments.

If you must use a credit card, set up text alerts through your credit card company to send you a message when your spending approaches what you have in your lifestyle bucket (more on that in the next chapter), and pay it off in full every month. And consider any previous credit card debt (from before you implemented this system) as part of your overhead or "must pay" expenses.

I hope you see how much easier it is to simply use a debit card.

Know First, Decide Second

You may have been advised at some point to run your finances like a business. This is good advice, to a point, but there is one critical difference. When a business adds an overhead expense (when it takes on an additional bill), the goal is to generate more revenue. A new building, a new employee, a new marketing program—all of these are intended to generate more money for the business. Adding to your personal overhead expenses, however, never generates extra revenue. You are simply adding monthly expenses, eating up your income.

Every time I have this conversation with a client, it seems like all they can hear is, "Don't buy a boat." Just because my Scandinavian skin burns in four minutes on the water doesn't mean I don't want *you* to have a killer boat. The message I need you to hear is that *too many people buy boats when their finances aren't able to handle it.*

Don't add additional overhead until you have a firm grasp on your current overhead. Focus on income first, overhead second, and your goals and ideals above all—that is the money recipe for intentional living.

Imagine making astute choices that reduce your lifestyle expenses (in ways you won't even miss) and let you put more money into future spending. Your options are still wide open. You could spend that money soon—on a vacation, a new car, or a year off—or you could put the money toward paying off your house (which would also reduce your overhead spending) or funding Future You. How would that feel?

The goal of the Year Off Money System is to help you shift your money from the left (overhead bucket) into lifestyle, and eventually further, into future spending—to the right. This will accomplish two things to help you get to your year of freedom as fast as possible: 1) You will have more free income in the future, and 2) You will need less money on a day-to-day basis, because you will have less overhead (and less lifestyle spending). The next chapter will walk you through exactly how to set up your own buckets and build a system that will let you take your own year off.

Future You is already thanking you.

Chapter 3 Accountability
CHECKLIST

Income Bucket

1. Complete the Consider Your Income Bucket and list all of your household income: predictable and semi-predictable income.

Overhead Bucket

2. Complete the Calculate Your Overhead Bucket exercise and make a list of all your overhead expenses. These are the regular payments necessary to run your life.

Future Spending Bucket

3. Complete the List Your Future Accounts exercise to find out how much money you're leaving for "Future You."

Lifestyle Bucket

4. Complete the Estimate Your Lifestyle Expenses exercise to calculate approximately how much money you are spending monthly to support your standard of living.

Your Buckets

5. Complete the Your Expense Percentages exercise to get a better idea of where your money is going.

6. Complete the Your Final Bucket Snapshot exercise and take a look at the total picture.

Accountability Partner

7. Go over the exercises from this chapter with your AP so they can check your math and cheer you on!

CHAPTER 4

Setting Up Your YO System

“A Mohr Furniture card, seriously?” I asked my new clients as they sat across the table from me. We had been going through all their credit accounts for about fifteen minutes now, and it seemed like there was no end in sight.

"Well, they gave us ten percent off of the purchase price, so it seemed like a good deal."

Doing some quick math in my head, I realized they had paid $750 in interest expense over the last several years to save $250 when they bought the couch. That didn't sound like a good deal to me.

"And how about your bank accounts?" I asked.

"We have our main checking and savings, and then we opened up another checking at the credit union where we got our car loan, plus we each kept our own separate checking accounts from before we were married."

"Is that all?"

"Yes. Well, besides the little balances that are in PayPal, Cash App, Venmo, and things like that, of course."

No wonder budgeting can be so hard! Today's technology and easy, instant financing are simple to use and hard to resist. When your money is scattered into a million pieces like this, however, it becomes difficult to manage.

Luckily, it's not that hard to organize and streamline your accounts. You just have to know what you're working with. This chapter will help you track down every last piece of your financial puzzle so you can put the whole thing to good use, both for your year off and for the future.

Preparing to Implement the System

When was the last time you actually synced all your accounts and looked at the totals? Maybe you've tried software or built a fancy spreadsheet while you were bored at work. Odds are, you have tried several strategies along the way but aren't doing any of them right now. That means you are probably using the most common strategy I know: managing money by watching your checking account balance (if you check it at all).

Another common method is to stop looking at your balance altogether toward the end of the pay period and start using a credit card. It's a clever way to never run out of money in your bank account, because there is always more credit! The problem with this seat-of-your-pants method is that it's too easy to stress-spend or live far beyond your means and mess up your future.

To set you up for your year, we need a different process. Something simple, sustainable, and easy to use. The stress, the worry, and the disorganization aren't going to go away overnight, but I promise they will go away if you follow my system.

Let's begin!

Clean Up Your Digital Trash

Our tendency to acquire more "stuff" as we move through life is well documented. Did you realize you are doing the same thing in the digital world?

If you're anything like me, your financial transactions from last week may have looked something like this:

- Bought groceries on the debit card
- Utility bill was auto-deducted from checking
- Business travel hit the business credit card
- Paid the babysitter with a money transfer app
- Used PayPal to buy an inappropriate T-shirt on eBay for my buddy turning forty
- Wrote a physical check to the kids' school for registration (because primary education hasn't discovered online banking in my part of the country yet)
- Bought lunch at the cash-only burger joint across the street from my office
- Bought an Americano at Starbucks using the Starbucks app, reloaded, of course, with Apple Pay
- Plugged a parking meter downtown with change (yes, we can operate a vehicle on Mars by remote control but we're still using change to park on Earth)

The irony is that having an endless parade of payment options makes your life easier in the moment but more difficult to track later. Simplification is our goal, but your current reality may be massive confusion. How are you supposed to manage your money buckets when your financial life is as scattered as mine was?

Most of us have over a hundred login accounts at random websites that we signed up for and only logged into once or twice. While an old username and password at Pets.com probably isn't hurting you, having financial accounts spread far and wide across the internet and your life does create problems.

Consider your 401(k) accounts. If you've held a few jobs, then you likely left one retirement account behind at each employer like a trail of breadcrumbs. Closing old banking and investment accounts can be a pain, so we often just let them hang out there in the ether.

Here are a few examples of unnecessary money accounts that are often forgotten about:

- Old store credit cards you opened to get 15 percent off
- Your first checking or savings account from wherever your parents bank
- Bank accounts in other states where you used to live
- 401(k) or other work retirement accounts from former jobs
- Weird old savings bonds your grandparents gave you for college

These accounts are a reminder of your sloppy money management, and they aren't good for your credit report.

I have never had a client complain that their financial life has become too simple. If you are ready to bring some intentionality into your life, prepare for that new chapter by closing up old accounts, consolidating your money, and cleaning up your digital trash.

Find a Good Bank or Credit Union

Remember the lady with the envelopes? That's what we're *not* going to do. The secret sauce of the YO System is to organize your bank account structure to match the spending categories you defined in the last chapter. Once you do that, managing your money well becomes as easy as looking at your checking account balance.

To implement this system, you need to put your money somewhere reliable, where it's safe and where it can work for you. This means finding a good bank or credit union.

What makes for a good bank? It's very simple: a good bank is one that doesn't try to sell you something other than banking services. Financial institutions that are involved in too many activities tend to not do anything well, so beware of a bank that wants to run your entire financial life. I am a fan of regional banks and local credit unions, which tend to have lower fees and higher interest rates.

The Income Account

Your Income Account is a single checking account that takes in and holds all your earnings and other incoming money (alimony, child support, etc.)—everything that went into your Income Bucket from the previous chapter. You may be able to repurpose an existing checking account, but most people simply open a new one.

To set up your income account, you will need to arrange direct deposit for your paychecks and other income to flow directly into this account. If you have a side hustle or pull earnings from your company, that should also drop right into this account. You want to put your good money habits on autopilot by automating as much of your new money system as possible.

If you have a significant other and share finances, you will both need to deposit directly into this account. If you never got around to combining your individual checking accounts, it's time to ditch them. The goal here is a financially successful household. That means all of the household income and overhead needs to run through the same system.

Your Income Account

- is a checking account (joint account for couples or combined households)
- is the place for all earnings and income, from any source, to be deposited
- does not require a debit card
- is not used to pay lifestyle expenses
- may need to be set up for direct deposit

Overhead Expenses

Remember that the Overhead Bucket held your non-optional bills and expenses like your mortgage, car, phone, and utilities. The total in this bucket shows you how much money it takes to run your household.

Income Account

Overhead Expenses
- Set up everything possible on autopay
- Set up everything else on bill pay
- NOT a separate account, overhead is paid from Income Account.

Mortgage	$1,800
Utilities	$300
Car Payment	$350
Internet/TV	$125
Auto Insurance	$185
Student Loan	$130
Other Debt Payments	$650
Cell Phone	$250
Gym Membership	$85

To keep it simple, your Overhead Bucket is not going to reside in a separate checking account. Rather, this collection of expenses will simply be paid from the Income Account you just set up. Automatically. The flow is this: all income enters the Income Account, and your overhead gets paid directly from there, *before anything else happens to the money.* Then, because you did the math in Chapter 3 to figure out what percentage of your money goes to overhead, you already know approximately what will be left in your Income Account after your bills are paid!

To set this account up, you want to ensure that all the overhead expenses you listed are set to pay out of this account. Since these bills are not optional, this strategy will guarantee they get paid.

You typically have four methods available for paying your bills out of your Income Account. They are listed here from most desirable to least desirable:

1. **Recurring Bill Pay.** All overhead expenses with a consistent monthly amount can be set up on recurring bill pay. Connecting your mortgage, car payments, and other large expenses this way allows them to be paid automatically, while you retain the

control to change these amounts by simply logging into your online bank account.

2. **Autopay.** Some of your big overhead expenses, like your utility bill, will have a different total due each month; you can't set up a fixed recurring autopay for $250 when it's going to be $308 next month. For these bills, set up autopay for the total amount directly with the company.

3. **One-Time Bill Pay.** If any of your overhead payments don't offer their own bill pay or autopay option, log in to your bank and pay this expense through bill pay as they come in. My city water bill is like this, so I log in and pay it monthly.

4. **Checks.** Old-school, baby! If you get desperate, checks are a method of last resort. (Let's hope we're done with checks in the next few years.)

Your Overhead Expenses
- are paid out of your Income Account
- include all non-optional "overhead" bills
- are set up to pay as automatically as possible

The Lifestyle Account

Recall from the previous chapter that your lifestyle expenses are where you live your life. These are your expenses by choice: groceries, gas, travel, entertainment, and excessive amounts of decorative pillows. All of these lifestyle expenses will now run through your new Lifestyle Account.

Most people convert their existing primary checking account into the Lifestyle Account. Set up a new checking account or convert an old one, and make sure you and others in your household have debit cards for this account.

Once you have this account up and running, take the total amount of Lifestyle Expenses you calculated in the previous chapter and set up a monthly transfer from your Income Account to your Lifestyle Account for that amount.

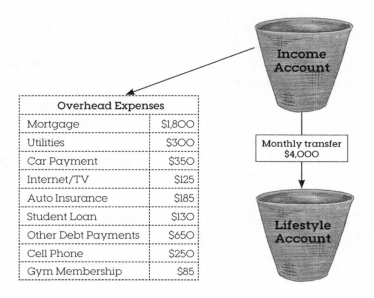

Overhead Expenses	
Mortgage	$1,800
Utilities	$300
Car Payment	$350
Internet/TV	$125
Auto Insurance	$185
Student Loan	$130
Other Debt Payments	$650
Cell Phone	$250
Gym Membership	$85

After that, you will use your debit card to access this account. And the best part? Your debit cards will never let you spend more than what is in this account, and you can spend this account down to $0 every single month and never feel guilty! The Lifestyle Account is designed for spending like a drunken sailor, right up until it's gone.

How is this possible? By the time you whip out your debit card to make a purchase, you have already been responsible with your money. You have paid your overhead expenses. Your contributions to Future You have already been made (more on that in the next section).

Your Lifestyle Account is for living. Spend it all every month, save a little for a shopping spree next month; it doesn't matter. Whatever you do, you can see how you are doing throughout the month by taking a quick peek at the account balance.

Your Lifestyle Account
- is a checking account (joint for couples)
- has a debit card for spending
- is not used to pay overhead (bills)

- receives a monthly transfer (or twice a month with your paycheck) from your Income Account
- is set up for all your money apps to draw from
- can be run down to zero every month

Congratulations! You have set up your three main money buckets from Chapter 3 in fully functional bank or credit union accounts. Your income, overhead, and lifestyle buckets have become your Income Account (which pays for your overhead) and your Lifestyle Account, and everything is set up to flow in the way that makes the most sense. This first part of the system is the core of the YO System. It takes care of your daily money management, and it will treat your money right.

Just by taking these first steps, you have already simplified your daily money life. You have created a way to limit the kind of spending that can get out of hand so easily: lifestyle expenses. Now you can easily check your Lifestyle Account balance to see what you have left to spend each month. No more mystery!

But this is only the first part of the system. Now, let's leap into the somewhat more challenging area of taking care of your future spending—which includes saving for your year off!

Your Future Spending Accounts

Now that Current You is on a sustainable money management system that only requires two bank accounts, all that's left to take care of is Future You! Remember, Future You is still *you*, so don't screw yourself over here. Not putting money toward Future You is like giving yourself a mandatory pay cut down the road. You don't deserve that!

Look back to those "Future You" buckets you listed in Chapter 3. During that exercise, we lumped your "Spend Soon" and "Spend Later" buckets together to get the total amount. Now it's time to look at these lists as the separate buckets they really are: the bucket that takes care of Future You, and the bucket that makes your time off possible.

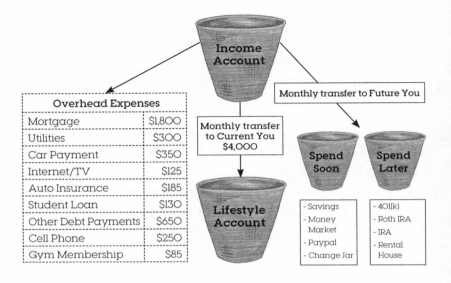

Overhead Expenses	
Mortgage	$1,800
Utilities	$300
Car Payment	$350
Internet/TV	$125
Auto Insurance	$185
Student Loan	$130
Other Debt Payments	$650
Cell Phone	$250
Gym Membership	$85

Income Account

Monthly transfer to Future You

Monthly transfer to Current You $4,000

Lifestyle Account

Spend Soon

Spend Later

Spend Soon	Spend Later
- Savings	- 401(k)
- Money Market	- Roth IRA
	- IRA
- Paypal	- Rental House
- Change Jar	

Year Off Account

Most people I work with are trying to save money to "spend soon" for one reason or another. Whatever the reason, I encourage my clients to consolidate all the money they want to spend over the next several years into one account. This is your "spend soon" bucket from the previous chapter, and it will become the account used to fund your year off (your Year Off Account, obviously).

How soon will you be spending the money in your Year Off Account? We'll calculate your year off date in the next chapter, but the goal is to spend that money on *you*, on *your* living expenses during your break. For now, take all the random money you have hanging out in the universe and consolidate it into one place—*one*. The collection of random accounts I see my clients leave unattended are unique and amazing (in a bad way)!

Here is an incomplete list of accounts that you may be on the lookout for:

- Savings accounts
- Money market accounts

- Certificates of deposit (CDs)
- Balances in random money apps
- Cash under the mattress (or a coffee can in the backyard)
- IOUs from friends
- That uncollected Super Bowl bet from your brother-in-law
- Unused gift card balances
- Gold or silver coins (though you can't remember where they came from)
- A jar full of two-dollar bills from your grandma

For now, deposit this money wherever is most convenient. We will put it to work for you later. You can use a savings account at your bank, or you can hide it under your mattress. My preferred place for my year off money is a short-term investment account.

(Investment strategies to maximize your Year Off Account will be covered in more detail in Chapter 7, but let's not complicate your beautiful money system with long words like "investments" yet. Just put it somewhere safe, and don't use it for anything else.)

Future You Account

It's sometimes hard to strike a balance between taking care of yourself and looking out for those who are closest to you. In addition to your family, offspring, and close friends, there is another important person whom you need to take care of: Future You. This person is going to be very, very mad at you if you don't strike a balance *now* between two competing issues:

1. Future You does not want regrets from not having done things, so you need to spend money now to live a full life (including taking this amazing time off to focus on yourself).
2. Future You is tired, has a few medical issues, and doesn't want to work so hard anymore, so you need to save money to support Future You.

Few things suck the air out a room faster than talking about retirement and investments. To ramp up the pain, we could talk about taxes and life insurance too. But don't worry: your retirement, insurance, and tax situation are not central to this year off process. I will provide more guidance for you in these areas later in the book, but for now, focus on how much money you can add to your Year Off Account.

That said, if you have the option, I strongly advise you to contribute to your 401(k) up to what your company will match. Every adult should also have a Roth IRA, so keep that contribution going as well (or plan on opening an account).

People who attend my workshops think the first step toward saving is to calculate how much money they will need in the future, but they are already missing an important step. You can't save for the future until you know how much money you need or are spending *today*. Now that you are implementing the YO System, you will know how much money you need for your year off *and for Future You*.

Set It Up and Enjoy the Ride

Well, things just got real, and at this point, it's understandable if you're feeling a bit of information overload. I have asked you to open accounts, close accounts, and change the way you've managed and even thought about money for a while now. It can feel like a lot. And you're not alone.

A couple I recently worked with found doing this work very difficult. In my office, when we used my system to map out their income, overhead, and lifestyle expenses, they finally understood where their money was going. I could see the reduction of stress and anxiety on their faces. It was awesome!

When it came time to implement the system, however, they delayed opening their new Income Account and setting up the automatic bill payments. Several months later, they were back in my office with the same problems, and unsure why they still couldn't track their money.

I told them that visualizing their money in buckets is the easy part. *The magic happens when you set up your accounts and transfers to match how you are now thinking about your money.* They didn't make the same mistake twice. After implementing the steps in this chapter, the stress and anxiety they were experiencing never returned.

Once this system is in place, all you have to do is glance at your Income Account to know everything you need to know about your financial life. You won't have to wade through hundreds of eight-dollar transactions to see where your money is going. Your Income Account will have fifteen or twenty transactions each month, and it will tell you:

- How much income you are making
- What your overhead expenses are
- How much money you are spending on your lifestyle
- What you are setting aside for Future You

It really is that simple. My wife and I don't even discuss what goes on in our Lifestyle Account. I don't care if that account is run down to $0 every month or if half of that goes to salons and hipster wine bars. All our conversations now revolve around the Income Account—always. Are we making more money now? What is our overhead, and can we reduce it? Are we running out of the Lifestyle Account early every month, and if so, how can we fix it?

When we implemented this system over ten years ago, being able to look at *one* account with minimal transactions and instantly know what is and isn't working for us was a game changer for our financial life— and for our marriage. As a bonus, I can also check exactly how many months I can take off work *without affecting our lifestyle.*

Now that you've gotten the Year Off Money System set up, in the next chapter, we'll figure out your first estimate of how long it will be until you can take a chunk of time off too.

Chapter 4 Accountability
CHECKLIST

Preparing for the Year Off Money System

1. Close extra/unnecessary accounts.

2. Find a good bank or credit union. Decide where you will do your banking. If you like your bank, you can keep your bank. If not, start researching potential regional banks or credit unions to move your money to.

Income Account

3. Income Account: Open a new checking account. In your online banking, nickname this account "Income Account."

4. Direct Deposit: Switch all of your direct deposits and income to automatically go into your Income Account.

Overhead Expenses

5. Overhead Payments: Set up all of your overhead expenses to get paid out of your Income Account.

Lifestyle Account

6. Set up two monthly transfers from your Income Account to your current checking account, which is now called the "Lifestyle Account." If your monthly lifestyle number is $4,000, then set up automatic transfers of $2,000 on the 1st and the 15th.

(continue)

Chapter 4 Accountability
CHECKLIST

Future Spending Accounts

7. Consolidate your "spend soon" accounts into your Year Off Account. Any balance that isn't a checking account or retirement account needs to be consolidated in one place, typically a savings or money market account.

8. Maintain (and keep contributing to) a Future You account to take care of yourself in retirement age.

Accountability Partner

9. Send a note to your AP that includes the following:

   • One bank where you will be conducting banking moving forward

   • A list of accounts (if any) that you need to close

   • The date by which you will have your Income and Lifestyle Accounts set up

CHAPTER 5

Calculating Your Year Off Date

Julie really wanted to go back to school. She was working part-time as a receptionist in a doctor's office, and it felt unlikely to her that answering phones and collecting urine samples was her purpose in life. Julie didn't hate her job; she wasn't desperate to get out. Her job paid well and contributed about 40 percent to the total income of her household. And when Julie and her husband met with me, they had no idea when—or if—they'd be able to make the change.

They did know one thing, though. Julie had always wanted to be a teacher. She and her husband had calculated that if she left her job and went to school full time, she could be certified and likely employed in a teaching position within twelve months. They had started to implement part of the Year Off Money System without realizing it: finding a meaningful career! Now they just had to figure out when they could afford to make the switch.

I taught them the rest of the YO System so they could finish organizing their financial lives, and when they came back into my office for an update, an amazing thing happened. Because of the work they had already done to categorize their money and anticipate future expenses, it didn't take long to calculate that Julie could go back to school and change careers without wreaking havoc on their lifestyle in just a couple of years.

And that was just a first estimate. We worked together to lower their overhead, pay off a few useless credit cards, and keep their lifestyle spending consistent. These changes cut their timeline down by almost nine months.

Before our meeting, Julie was resigned to a lifetime of test tubes and scheduling software. Now, with her year off date in hand, she was on her way to a new, rewarding career.

Julie proved that once you have a handle on your income, overhead, lifestyle, and future spending accounts, you can move forward with any life plan you like. Your plan can be as simple or as ambitious as you want it to be. Just like Julie's—Julie is currently enrolled in college for this fall semester and following her dream of becoming an elementary school teacher.

Wherever you're starting from—no matter how unlikely it may seem—implementing the YO System you learned in the last chapter allows you to stick to your spending plan, and save consistently and steadily for your year off. Now, using all that information we've collected, let's calculate exactly when your year can begin!

Gathering Your Data

Finding and creating purpose and meaning in your life is a key part of this process, possibly the most important thing you can do. But if you find that your purpose and your money-management skills are still a flaming dumpster fire wreaking havoc on your life, a simple sabbatical won't fix it. You didn't pick up this book because you wanted a temporary break from the insanity. You are still reading because you are ready for permanent change that can carry you through this season of your life and into the next one.

EXERCISE:
Calculate Your Desired Monthly Income

Look back at your real overhead and lifestyle costs from Chapter 3 and add them together to find the total monthly income you'll need to maintain your current needs.

Overhead	+ Lifestyle	= Desired Monthly
$...............	$...............	Income $...............

There you go! That's the amount you'll rely on each month during your year off.

A note about estimated expenses: This exercise assumes that you're planning on staying where you are now: same rent or mortgage, same lifestyle. If you're planning to leave your hometown, do as much research and talk to as many people as you possibly can to get a realistic expectation of what you'll spend. This exercise might introduce some complications, but careful upfront planning will help you avoid nasty surprises that could cut your time short.

With that in mind, let's answer a few simple questions and create your first estimate of how long it will take for you to reach twelve full months of freedom.

What Do You Need?

When you take time off and the income stops rolling in, how much money will you need to keep paying the bills? This isn't the time to estimate what you *think* you would spend if you took a year off. Use what you spend *right now*, in reality.

Luckily, we already did the hard work in earlier chapters, and you know exactly what that number is.

EXERCISE:
Look at Your Monthly Contributions

If you've gone through the exercises in the previous chapter, you've already carved out a monthly amount to move into your Year Off Account to increase the balance even faster. (If not, start now; anything you contribute regularly can shave months or even years off your year off date!)

Look at the total balance in your Year Off Account, and write the number below along with the amount you contribute monthly to that account.

Year Off Account: $...

Monthly Year Off Account Contribution: $................................

That's it! Now you have all of the information you need to calculate your year off date.

What Do You Have?

Great, now how are you going to replace that income? Here is where you put your Year Off Account to work. Add up all the money you were able to gather from your savings, money market, and random cash accounts into your Year Off Account and count it as money you are holding to spend during that year.

That number, too, can change; the idea is to get that money to grow. More on that later.

Starting the Countdown to Your Year Off

Before we crunch the numbers and look at your very first year off date, a few words of warning.

EXERCISE:
Calculate the Number of Months Until Freedom

Remember, the number you see is simply an opening bid based on what your life looks like *today*. In a sense, it's the worst possible outcome.

Now, let's calculate your year off date!

	YOU	Example
Year Off Income: Monthly Income to Replace x 12	$.............	$72,000
Then subtract	-	-
Year Off Account Current Balance	$.............	$18,000
Equals Amount of Money Still Needed for Your Year Off	$.............	$54,000
Then Divide By	/	/
Monthly Year Off Account Contribution	$.............	$750
Equals	=	=
Number of Months to Freedom	....	72

There you go!

Remember, it's okay to not like the first number you see here. It is not uncommon for me to help people go from five or more years to under eighteen months in short order. You have the power to shorten your waiting period dramatically if you choose to.

I still have a few tricks up my sleeve to drastically move up your year off date. In Chapter 7, I will show you how to reduce this number, possibly even to a fraction of what you see above. (In the example above, my clients were able to get their year off date down from seventy-two months to *eighteen months*. Does that sound better?)

Before I show you the tricks we used to increase their money skills (and their happiness and freedom), we first want to make sure that Future You doesn't get the shaft on your journey to discover who Current You wants to be.

Most people who complete this exercise for the first time are shocked by their initial timeline for taking a year off—and *not* in a good way. If you don't like the first number you see, don't be discouraged. There are several things you can do to reduce what you need each month and move your year off date closer to reality. I'll discuss several of them in the coming chapters, so hang in there!

When I first determined my year off date, it was fourteen months away. I have helped others who were only four months away and some who were ten years away. You may be one of the lucky ones who is under a year away from a life-altering experience, but that isn't the most common timeline. Your initial calculations may show that your time off is several *years* away.

Regardless of when your year off date is scheduled to begin, it's important to remember one thing: *that date will change.* Your income will go up, you will be watching your expenses more closely (and reducing your spending where you can), and your savings account will grow and make money. As you're about to learn, the future is in your hands!

Taking Care of Future You

Once your mind fully latches onto the idea of a year off, you will likely start to identify a few shortcuts and strategies in everyday life to get you there faster. This is a good thing: everything you can do to shave off unnecessary expenses and contribute more to your Year Off Account helps to shrink the wait time.

But there's one bucket that needs to stay off-limits, and that's the bucket you're building to cover that longer time off from your income: the bucket you're reserving for Future You.

What About My "Spend Later" Money?

Recently, I was working with a client who had implemented the YO System to perfection and was rapidly moving her year off date closer. One day she called me, thrilled that she had found an unexpected chunk of money. The day before, she'd received a statement in the mail from a previous employer for an old 401(k) she had forgotten about. The balance was $20,000! She figured that this money would move her year off date up almost four full months and wanted to know what I thought.

Unfortunately, I had to deliver some bad news: *all retirement money counts as Spend Later money and may not be used to finance your time away from your job.* Remember, you don't want to screw over Future You twenty years down the road just to shave a few months off of your year off date.

And it isn't just Future You that misses out; cashing out your retirement accounts can cost you in other ways as well. If my client had requested a check for the $20,000 in her retirement account, she would have received only $14,000. Approximately 30 percent would have gone straight to taxes and penalties. That is money you don't need to lose today.

The bottom line here is that any money you have put aside for spending much later—especially funds that would trigger big taxes and penalties upon withdrawal, like work retirement funds, IRAs, or cash in life insurance policies—are off-limits. Trust me: by following the YO System, you can take your break without them.

The year off process is about more than a search for significance. It's about setting you up for the rest of your life. Looking back, the positive habits I developed leading up to my year off ended up being the most valuable part of my journey. Regardless of what I discovered with my time off, the financial and personal discipline it took to get here became habits that will last a lifetime.

My client may have been unable to use that "surprise" money for her year off, but the discipline of leaving it invested when she wanted so badly to spend it will pay even bigger dividends for her down the road.

Should I Stop Contributing to Future Me?

Later in this book, you will see the acceleration power of shifting even a few hundred dollars out of your overhead expenses into your Year Off Account. Living on less and putting aside more is a tool that will drastically speed up your path toward freedom. This new focus on identifying extra money every month often leads people to the same place: the retirement account contributions that come out of every paycheck.

Don't go toward the light!

Cutting the amount withheld from your paycheck and moving that money to your Year Off Account can be very tempting, but resist. Each Future You account will play an important role later in your life during that longer break from work called "retirement," and it's important not to be shortsighted in your management of these treasures.

Here are a few accounts you may have (along with a bit of advice that Future You will thank you later for following).

- **401(k).**

More likely than not, your 401(k) gives you free money up to a certain amount: if you put in $100, your employer puts in $100 as well. *Take it.* Take everything you can of this free money match. You can't go back and get free money from your company later, so take the paycheck deduction that maximizes that free money now.

- **Roth IRA.**

I heart Roth IRAs, and you should too. When this book was printed, Roth IRA accounts offered one of your few options in life to accumulate *tax-free money.* Yes, that's right: Roth IRAs are filled with money that will never be taxed again! You will want a large amount of this type of money later in life, so don't ignore it now. Every adult should be contributing something to a Roth IRA, even if means a small delay in leaving your job for a while. It's that important to Future You.

- **"Other" Investment Accounts.**

Here is where you can be a bit more flexible. If you have any balances in random, *non-retirement* investment accounts, you should have consolidated those balances into your Year Off Account in Chapter 4 along with any monthly contributions. One often-missed place where money might be hiding, however, is the automatic payroll deduction you may have set up to buy company stock at a discount. Your company may be great, but aren't you still reading because you might not want to work there anymore? Feel free to repurpose this money into your Year Off Account, and use the proceeds from selling any company stock you may have already purchased to turbocharge your Year Off Account.

- **Life Insurance.**

Insurance should have its own chapter, but I respect you way too much to put you through that. Suffice it to say that while it's certainly important to cover your bases and protect your family from an unpredictable future—more on that later—you shouldn't look at life insurance as a way to grow your wealth. I'm amazed at the number of people who think they are "saving money" in a life insurance policy. If your life insurance statement says you have a "cash value," you can likely put that money to better use. Use the information in Chapter 8 to find a fiduciary financial planner who can help you see the light and repurpose this money.

Do I Need an Emergency Fund?

Here's the thing: I do not believe in "emergency" or "reserve" accounts. They are dead money that slow you down from accomplishing your financial goals.

The only true emergency should be a replacement of income . . . which the entire Year Off Money System is built to solve. And after building your safety net according to the steps laid out in Chapter 8, unexpected events like medical expenses or new water heaters should not derail this system.

It can be difficult to put away money for the future if you think in terms of emergencies, but if you think about it, this book is all about building one giant emergency fund. And isn't it more exciting to save if you think in terms of freedom rather than disaster?

Don't Be Discouraged!

When I first started planning my year off, I wanted it to start the next day. I imagine you are in a similar boat. Transferring your time, talents, and energy to something more important to you—and presumably to the world—sounds incredible, and the time between now and then feels like forever.

So I started looking for ways to accelerate my timeline. But I had to face a hard truth: I actually wasn't ready for my time off yet. If I had been able to start the next day, I can now see that it would have been a miserable failure. I didn't have the habits, the discipline, or the vision to make the most of my time.

As I sit here typing this, I am only a few months into my year off. I can safely say that even with all the tools I developed in preparation for this year, having virtually unlimited time for myself is immensely overwhelming. The systems in this book are designed to eliminate the overwhelm and confusion that come with too many options, which leads to running in place instead of moving forward with a purpose.

I see it over and over again: as you develop the habits and discipline required to make this work, your year off date magically accelerates until it is sprinting toward you at a breakneck pace. Only it isn't magic. It's you, taking more and more control of your future (and your present) every day. It's you, organizing your accounts exactly the way I've laid out for you in this book. It's you, coming up with your own ways to put away a little more money each month.

Remember, the year off date you calculated earlier in the chapter is just an opening bid. If you put in the work, your date with destiny will literally meet you partway. Keep checking things off the checklists and checking in with your accountability partner!

In the next chapter, we will explore new habits for success that you can start to build now during your wait time. Then, once you've set yourself up with the habits that will move you toward your goal, we will work on accelerating your year off date in Chapter 7.

Trust the system, and trust yourself. You'll get there—and by the time you do, you'll be ready.

Chapter 5 Accountability
CHECKLIST

What Do You Need?

1. Complete the Calculate Your Desired Monthly Income exercise by adding your monthly overhead and lifestyle expenses together to get the amount of money you need to live on every month during your time off. Multiply by the number of months you want to take off. That's your nut to crack!

What Do You Have?

2. Complete the Look at Your Monthly Contributions exercise to calculate the amount of money you have available in your Year Off Account and determine how much money you can add to your Year Off Account every month.

Starting the Countdown

3. Complete the Calculate the Number of Months until Freedom exercise by using the formula presented in the chapter to calculate year off date! (Don't panic: this number is only your first estimate.)

Future You

4. Double-check on your contributions to your Future You (retirement) accounts.

5. Make sure you are contributing to your company's 401(k) enough to get any free money match.

6. Do you have a Roth IRA?

7. Did you find any non-retirement accounts that you can add to your Year Off Account?

(continue)

Chapter 5 Accountability
CHECKLIST

Accountability Partner

8. Send a message to your AP with your year off date. Include both a frowny face and a smiley face ... because your date might be too far away, but you are about to move it up drastically.

CHAPTER 6

While You Wait: Preparing for Your New Life

"**B**ut I'm ready *now*," Mike grumbled yet again.

Mike worked a government job, hated his manager, and dreamed of the day he wouldn't have to take crap from his power-hungry bosses on a daily basis. He was all in for taking a serious break.

Every time we met at my office, he would show up with his blue file folder full of new ideas on how he could reduce an expense here, put away another dollar there, and generally get the hell out of his job as quickly as possible. We were able to use the Year Off Money System to move his year off date closer, but there was one future event that blocked us from moving the date any closer than twenty-four months out.

Mike was about to turn forty-eight, and he was eligible for a pension at age fifty. Waiting two more years would provide him with a lifetime monthly payment of $4,000 from his suddenly-less-annoying government job. On top of that, his wife had just quit her job, and he had a kid in college and mortgage payments to make. The math just didn't work without waiting. Mike knew there wasn't much he could do but ride out the system until his pension kicked in, but he wasn't thrilled.

And to a point, he was right: because of the work he had already put in, his money was starting to run like a well-oiled machine. His new accounts were set up, he knew exactly how much money he had to spend on different aspects of his life, and the balance in his Year Off Account kept climbing. On paper, he *was* ready. But he was so eager to get out of his old life that he hadn't stopped to consider what he'd do in his new one.

From our earlier talks, I knew that Mike was almost entirely focused on *when* he could get out of his job; I hadn't heard a lot about *what* he'd do when he got there. I also knew that if he didn't take his preparations for his time off seriously, Mike could experience the same issues that I'd seen many older retirees face when they left a long-term job: boredom, health issues, irritating their spouse, and suddenly thinking they can manage their own investments. Yikes!

I couldn't help but wonder if this two-year delay was just what Mike needed. He may have been on his way financially, but now it was time to get ready mentally—and Mike had a lot to prepare for.

Why do you really want to take a break? Why are you putting a career on hold and possibly inconveniencing your family and friends? Implementing the YO System for your finances is rewarding in itself, but preparing for the mental side of your time away is also endlessly satisfying and entertaining if you attack it head on.

At this point, it's important to have a clear understanding of your goals—for your year off and for the future. To make sure your plans and goals can sustain you through all the changes that lie ahead, let's take a moment to review them.

Mike is still two years away from his dream of changing careers. He knows a lot can change, and a lot can go wrong. In my experience, however, it rarely does go wrong, because my clients are more equipped than ever to meet new challenges as they arise.

If you are after a life of meaning and purpose, it's time to build the habits and skills that will get you there. In this chapter, I'll cover a handful of habits you can build and things you can do to set yourself up for an eye-opening year off.

Checking Your Why

Maybe you've known exactly what you want to do since you were a teenager and don't want to put it off any more. If so, you have a head start on the rest of us. If you are like me, however, you might be making more progress on a mental list of things you *don't* want to do than you are actually searching for the life you do want. Finding your destination can be an exercise in trial and error.

For example, Mike doesn't want change so he can build houses in Guatemala. He wants change because he hates his stupid job and his even stupider boss. This may lead Mike to Guatemala, where he might find immense satisfaction in building houses, but that isn't his main motivation for organizing his life.

There is nothing wrong with this. Sometimes, discovering why we are doing something starts with creating a big-ass list of things we *don't* want to do. Finding your purpose or meaning in your life—your *why*— won't happen just by sitting down and thinking about it. You can't create significance out of thin air.

You may not realize it, but you have spent your whole life building up preferences of things you do and don't want to spend your time on. Let's take an inventory of them so you know what habits you need to build prior to your time off.

Your Year Off Mission Statement

Remember that company picnic a few years ago, where your boss stood up on a table to announce your company's new mission statement? That mission probably went something like this: *We strive to do more of the things that are good for us while tirelessly working to eliminate the things that are bad for us.* Great advice—but I bet three months later you didn't remember what the mission statement said, and neither did your bosses.

Writing down a bunch of sparkly nonsense didn't help your company improve its game, and it won't help you. Everyone who embarks on this journey has the same mission: discovery and progress in a new direction. That's not the part you need to remember.

Instead of a mission statement, you need a living, breathing document to keep you focused on your *why*. You need something that will evolve over time as you enjoy certain experiences and vow to never have others again.

You may be out to discover whether your ideas for the future are good or need to be tossed in the recycle bin. You may be looking for new ideas for moving your life forward. Or you may be out to give back, full time. If you're still not clear on your *why* at this point, that's okay; that's what we'll figure out in this chapter.

I have found that the best way to start formulating a plan for finding your why is to make a list of all those things you *don't* want to do. This list is an accomplishment. Something is triggering your desire for change, so write it down while it's on your mind. And hopefully, that list leads you to another list of things you *do* want to do.

Here is an example of things you might not want in your life in the column on the left and how they can trigger ideas for what you do want in the column on the right.

Things I Don't Want	Things I Do Want
• Work for someone else	• Work with a team I respect and people who respect me
• Work on the weekends	• Flexibility with my schedule
• Have my phone on me 24/7	• Regularly work on new projects
• Sit in a cubicle	• Move locations during the day
• Work for a boss who makes excuses	• Casual dress
• Commute more than 20 minutes	

The Biggest Risk of All

While I was planning my own year off with my wife, she asked me if it was scary to leave behind everything I've known my whole adult life to try something different. I told her that yes, it was, but not half as scary as the alternative: waking up ten years from now and

EXERCISE:
Record Your Wants and Don't-Wants

Now it's your turn to make a brief list of things you *don't* want for your life in the column on the left. As you write, see if your answers generate ideas for things you *do* want, and list those things in the column on the right:

Things I Don't Want	Things I Do Want
1.	1.
2.	2.
3.	3.
4.	4.
5.	5.
6.	6.
7.	7.
8.	8.
9.	9.
10.	10.

If you need more space, grab another sheet of paper, and don't stop until you've let it all out! You paid a high price to discover all of the things you don't want to do with your life. Write them down, remember them, and never forget.

To shift your focus from the don't want to the do want column, you need a few more tools in your toolbox. The exciting news is that you can start today. You don't need to wait until your money is operating at full efficiency to start on the hard work it will take for you to plan a successful and meaningful year.

The next step is to develop a few good habits, decide how you're going to deal with your current job, and go public with your intent. Focusing on these areas will lay the groundwork for a successful time away. Even more importantly, it will make your waiting time more productive and meaningful.

In a sense, your year off begins now.

having a life of meaning just as out of reach as it was a decade before. Spending another ten years in the rut race, just because it's familiar, is the riskiest choice of all.

In my opinion, the biggest mistake people make is pursuing what they want *today*, because it's likely to change before they can even get there. Most of our wants are short term. We want stuff and status. When we look back, we can see that these wants were silly. Somehow, we forgot about our deeper, longer-term wants, the important things in life, like our dreams, our relationships, and helping others.

There are two types of regrets: things you should have done and things you shouldn't have done. The good news is that it isn't too late to take care of the more painful type of regret. Eliminating your future regrets won't happen by accident, however. It's time to get intentional about the story you want to be told about your life.

Your life can be far more fulfilling if you start by focusing on what it is you don't want. Here is what I came up with for myself:

Should Have Done

I definitely should have (but didn't and will totally regret if I never do):

• Spent more time with my family.

• Stayed in touch with old friends.

• Expressed my feelings to others.

• Let myself be happy and do what I enjoy (besides partying).

• Taught my children something awesome about life every day.

• Pursued my dreams when I had them (oh wait, I still have them!).

• Tried a different hobby, a new one that I have been longing to explore . . . like writing!

Shouldn't Have Done

I wish I could take back:

• Hurting the people I hurt.

• Being an asshole that one time for no reason. I'm sure it was just that once.

• The overalls I wore in Junior High.

• Accepting that dead-end job that wasted years of my life.

• Not speaking with a family member for several years.

• Not looking both ways before I pulled into traffic.

EXERCISE:
List Your Regrets

Conduct a little research online and you will come to the same conclusion I did: Most people, at the end of their lives, regret the things they wish they had done far more than the things they wish they had not done. You don't have to be one of them.

What does your list of regrets look like? Take a moment to brain-dump some ideas. This list will give you a whole new perspective on how your year off can help you build more meaning (and less regret) into your life.

What regrets don't you want to carry anymore? What are you doing now that you wish you weren't? Inside what you don't want, you will find those deeper, longer-term wants that are all too easy to forget.

Think about this for a moment, right now, and make a list of everything you wish you would have done differently.

Should Have Done	Shouldn't Have Done
I definitely should have	I wish I could take back

Shaking up your life routine may feel terrifying, and it's okay to be a little scared of it. But before you file this exercise in the "maybe someday" category and step right back into your rut, ask yourself which is the bigger risk: taking a chance on fixing your regrets now, or waking up ten years from now knowing that nothing has changed at all and likely never will?

The column on the right is carved in stone. We can't go back and undo what we've done; we can only make amends and move forward.

The column on the left is written in pencil. We can erase every single item on our list, one by one, until we feel at peace with a life well lived. We just have to choose to do it now.

Building Habits, Not Goals

"I want to climb Mount Everest!" Wow, cool—now what?

Saying things out loud is really easy; organizing your life to accomplish your goals can be really hard. Wanting to climb Mount Everest doesn't mean anything until you start arranging your life to make it happen. Once you start to look into it, however, you might realize that you simply wanted to learn to climb . . . and that you might need to set a different specific goal to accomplish it. (Like taking your first climbing lesson.)

Right now, your time off contains more unknowns than you may be comfortable with, but that is one thing that makes this experience so valuable. Your goals may have started out as climbing Mount Everest, but they can evolve; you might end up training to climb beautiful Mount Rainier instead (Pacific Northwest reference). As of today, you need to focus on building skills you can use to climb any mountain and habits you can use in any weather (or if you decide to take up scuba diving instead).

My point is this: goals change, but building habits to reach any goal is what makes you successful. Here are a few examples that demonstrate how developing habits will benefit you more over the long run than setting goals.

- If you want to get in shape, you could choose to lose ten pounds in the next two months (goal), or you could go on a walk every morning (habit). Only one of those options helps you over your lifetime.
- If you hate dealing with your car, you can vow to spend less than $250 a year in repair services (goal), or you can commit to getting your vehicles serviced several times a year (habit).

- If you want to spend more time with your kids, you could commit to taking them to a fancy Florida resort full of trademarked characters (goal), or you can work on eating dinner together as a family every night (habit).

Get the difference? Goals are fine, but they can just be one-hit wonders. A habit is a tangible, repeating action in the real world that benefits you over and over. Building effective habits will certainly lead you to accomplishing your goals, but they will continue serving you well after you reach those goals.

It's Easy: The Piggyback Method

According to research, the easiest way to introduce a new habit into your life is to tie the new behavior to something you already do. For example, if you want to read more, you could read for thirty minutes every evening after dinner. Eating dinner is a daily habit you are unlikely to break. Even if you forget to have it one night, you will probably be right back at it the next night, and you'll remember to pick up that book when you put down the fork.

That's how I found the time to work on projects in the afternoon. I discovered I was great at managing my time in the morning, but as the day wore on, I would get busy and stop moving any major initiatives forward. I solved this by adding a step to the morning routine I had already established (which I will cover in a minute).

At the end of my existing morning routine, I now have a new habit: find an empty block of time in my afternoon and schedule time to work on a project. Once it's on my calendar, it happens! Now, around 1:30 p.m. (or whenever I'm free that day), I can break away from whatever nonsense I am doing and switch gears to focus on a project. Without this new habit, afternoon productivity for me would be hit or miss (mostly miss). Now, it's as easy as showing up for a meeting on time.

Three Habits to Form Today

We always have room for improvement in our daily habits. Goals are great, up to a point. They are good for the short term. Positive habits, however, are what make the difference and keep us progressing in life. Habits can help us achieve those goals, and habits come with an additional bonus: once you develop them, they last a lifetime.

Here are three success habits you can get started on (or take to a new level) while you wait for your year off to begin.

Habit #1: Start a Morning Routine

A few years ago, here is what I used to do first thing in the morning: I rolled over in bed, picked up my phone, and immediately started checking my messages. If you have a full-time job, checking texts in the morning can lead to browsing your email. In bed! And let's not even start with Twitter. By this point, whatever plans you had for the morning have been delayed or disrupted, if not outright destroyed. Opening yourself to outside factors allows events around you to dictate your mood (and your to-do list) for the beginning of your day.

Eventually, I noticed that when I began my day without a schedule, it was difficult to wrestle back control of my day. I ran from one crisis to the next, returning emails, phone calls, and generally putting out fires.

However, everything changed once I developed a morning routine. Now when I wake up, I don't check my phone. I immediately go into morning mode without even thinking about it. By 7 a.m., I feel focused, I've been productive, and I still have most of the day left to listen to nineties rap.

Here is what my morning routine currently looks like:

1. Wake Up at 5:30 a.m.
2. Meditate – 5 min
3. Read Bible and Pray – 10 min
4. Review Planner, Schedule, and To-do List for Day – 5 min
5. Schedule Afternoon Project Time – 1 min

6. Make Coffee – 10 min
7. Writing Time – 60 min (this is how I wrote a book!)
8. Workout – 20 min

That's it! I am up and moving my personal life forward for almost two hours before I get into my work messages or emails, and by the time everything kicks in, I feel productive, calm, and confident that I am going to have a great day. Sure, the later events of the day will distract, sidetrack, and generally annoy me. But not in the morning. My morning habit ritual sets the tone for the whole day.

Script the first sixty to ninety minutes of your morning. Write it down and stick it on your bathroom mirror where anyone who sees it can make fun of you. At night, put a sticky note with your routine on your phone screen so you don't start checking it first thing in the morning. Spend your mornings on offense, not defense or avoidance. If you are responsible for getting your kids out the door in the morning, you may have to start earlier or shorten your routine, but you can still do it!

Developing a morning routine will ensure that every day of your year off feels good to you and begins exactly the way you want it to. If you are doing anything to avoid your life, you need to implement this system!

Habit #2: Start a Year Off Journal

There's a tired cliché that says life is a journey, not a destination. (Put another way, life is about the habits you develop, not the goals you set.) Your ideas of how you want to spend your year off are going to change dramatically, from your first tentative thoughts, to the day you begin your time off, to the end of your experience. You are going to grow and evolve in ways that are hard to predict. What seems important now may not be important at all by the time you are through. Wouldn't it be great to create a record of the discoveries you make along the way?

To get the most out of this time, put together a Year Off Journal (a YO Journal, of course). If traditional journaling is hard for you, that's okay. This journal is not a place to record your hopes and dreams for the future (although you can include and explore those). This document will serve as a centralized record of where you are, where you want to go, and what the hell you were thinking last week. It's a place to document your thought process about *why something seems like a good idea to explore right now*.

When I work on my journal, my goal is to leave a record of what the hell Past Me was thinking so Current Me can avoid repeating lessons I have already learned the hard way. My thoughts and aspirations about life are always evolving. My ambitions are growing in certain areas, but there are also areas where they are receding. What made sense twelve months ago doesn't make any sense to me now. I wasn't *wrong* a year ago, I was just *different*.

If you're like me and find it difficult to get started, try treating your YO Journal like a movie script where you are the protagonist. In your story, you are the main character, and your hero's journey awaits you. Over the course of a movie's story, you can see how the character has changed, how they come to see and do things they never could before.

Your YO Journal will have a beginning, and a middle, but no end. It will include obstacles you encountered along the way and the skills and habits you developed to overcome them. It will help you understand why the old you couldn't see things and why you prioritized things that didn't matter. Most importantly, it will help you make meaning out of your journey into and throughout your year off.

Habit #3: Find a To-Do List Process That Works for You

I'm at the grocery store, staring down the dairy aisle, milk and eggs in my basket. There is one more thing my wife told me to get, but for the life of me, I just can't remember what it is. I didn't write it down, because what kind of moron can't remember three things during a two-minute drive to the grocery store?

This moron, apparently. By the time I have driven the two minutes to the store, I have already thought of a new book idea, started three new businesses, composed three or four emails, and solved one major world problem. And now I can't remember the third item we need. Milk, eggs, and . . . ?

Maintaining a to-do system that works for you isn't just about making sure your errands are done well. It accomplishes two specific objectives:

1. **Flushes Your Mind.**

First, it gives you a way to get random things out of your head. You know what you need to get done and you don't want to forget it. Until you do. Or maybe it remains in your head to distract, disorient, and taunt you because you have to do something else first. Don't let that happen.

2. **Puts You in Charge.**

Second, this habit puts you in control of your day. Taking a break from your job is primarily about finding time to move projects forward and discover new experiences, but that doesn't mean the responsibilities of life are going to go away. You still have things that need to get done. Let's get 'em done.

Between projects, classes, meetings, or however you set up your year off, you get to choose how to spend your time: on your own goals and priorities or reacting to everyone else's stuff. Those choices will affect how happy you are with your results. After saving and managing your life like crazy to take this time for yourself, would you rather do what's a priority for you, or check your texts and emails and do what's important to others?

Five or ten items on a list don't look that scary, but keeping those same items in your head can make you feel like the world is spinning, and soon your brain starts forgetting a few to feel better. If this sounds familiar, you need a system for tracking your to-dos.

There is only one good system in the world: the one you use consistently. If you don't yet have a process that works for you, here are a few digital ideas for keeping to-do lists.

1. **Set Phone Reminders.** This works great because you can typically use it hands-free. Just ask your phone to remind you to do something, and it usually does.

2. **Use Your Phone Calendar.** If you don't like the clunky reminder app, you can always use the calendar feature. Advantages of this system include easier syncing across devices, ease of repeating tasks, sharing of tasks with family members, and the ability to schedule specific time to accomplish the task during the day.

3. **Find a Third-Party Task App.** The market is full of to-do list and reminder apps, and I imagine most of them work better than the built-in apps on your phone, but who has time to learn a new random app? This option may be for the perfectionist crowd.

Apps aren't your thing? Here are a few analog options you might consider.

1. **Use a Day Planner.** I don't see physical planners much anymore, but you won't see me mocking them. If digital solutions aren't working for you, go with paper.

2. **Use a Notebook.** More open-ended than a planner, a notebook is useful for people drowning in ideas throughout the day. If this is you, see if you can consolidate your notes and ideas in the same notebook.

3. **Use a Dry-Erase Board.** This was my parents' system. If something needed to be done—or, more commonly, if someone felt the urge to deliver unsolicited advice to a sibling—it would magically appear on the dry-erase board above the phone.

My preferred to-do list solution is a digital notebook on my computer. I keep my to-do list in the same place that I keep outlines for projects I am working on, jot down random ideas, and lay out my priorities for the week. It syncs across all of my devices, so it's available to me at home, at work, or when I'm out and about.

What I don't use it for, apparently, is grocery shopping. For that, I use standing in the middle of the store like an idiot and waiting for my wife to text me back. Milk, eggs, and . . . fabric softener. How could I forget that?

Now, What About That Job?

Let's talk about your job. Whether you are self-employed, middle management, a line worker, or CEO of a major corporation, dealing with your employment situation is going to be . . . well, difficult . . . and it's going to take time. This piece isn't a riddle that is going to be solved in one brainstorming session by yourself or in one conversation with your boss.

Luckily, you have some time to figure this out. But even if your year off date is still several months away, it's never too early to start working on your exit strategy.

Three Ways to Step Away

As a business owner, my year off strategy centered around training my employees. They had to take on more responsibilities, make more decisions by themselves, and generally take the next step in their careers whether they were ready for it or not. To make that possible, I had to transfer the procedures for my business from my head onto paper so they knew what to do.

Turning my business from a one-man-show into an entity that could function without my physical presence was the first tangible benefit of my year off process, and I didn't even have to wait for my year off! It was a project long overdue, and I didn't realize how poorly I had been managing things until I had a reason to get organized.

You may have career-related items you have been neglecting, too. Now is the time to clean them up. Let's look at three main ways you can deal with taking an extended break from your job.

Take a Sabbatical

Historically, a paid year off was reserved for tweeded-out college professors, but times they are a-changin'. More and more employers are offering employees a chance for paid time off to pursue meaningful activities. An even larger number of employers are offering unpaid time off with a guarantee that your job will be waiting for you when you return.

Being paid to do nothing sounds awesome, of course, but if your employer offers you an unpaid sabbatical, that's all you need for your time off. With the YO System, you're jump-starting your system for replacing your income, so even if you can't pull a paycheck, you can still rock your Year Off Account! According to the US Small Business Administration, however, nearly half the employees in America work for small businesses. I think it's safe to say that a formal sabbatical program is unlikely for nearly all of them.

Does that mean you can't take an extended break from your job if you work for a small business? Of course not. Just because there isn't an official program in place doesn't mean your employer isn't interested in hearing you out about an extended absence. (For one reason, it's expensive to replace you!) Employers don't want to say no; they want to say yes. You need to give them a reason to say yes.

Let me give you a quick management tip. When you walk into your boss's office and say, "I know our company doesn't offer a formal program for extended time off, but it's something I'm really interested in, and I'm hoping you'll be open to me taking some type of sabbatical next year," the words coming out of your mouth aren't what your boss hears. What your boss actually hears is, "I am going to do less work, which means you are going to do more. Now you have a bunch of extra things to figure out, including hiring a new employee, training them, and documenting all of the processes that I currently do." Who wants to say yes to that?

Framing what you are asking for as a *benefit* (as opposed to more work) for the company and for your boss is important. Offer to help explore new technology, properly document existing procedures, or cross-train other employees to handle your duties. Once you have implemented positive changes at your job that you can demonstrate to your boss, *then* you can approach her with your master plan.

What boss doesn't want more efficiency and better systems for their business? You won't know unless you ask. At least this approach will give you a fighting chance of convincing your employer that time off will benefit the company. And if it doesn't work, this next strategy might be the one for you.

Find a New Job

A year off doesn't have to be about changing your career. At its core, your decision to take a break is about upgrading your levels of joy and satisfaction. If you don't like your job—if it just pays the bills—then leave it. If you think you can live a more meaningful life in a different job, you owe it to yourself to look into it.

You certainly don't want to wrap up an amazing year by finding yourself unemployed, however. Holding tightly to your job is undoubtedly the best short-term financial advice, but so is buying secondhand underwear. Your year off—and more importantly your year off process—is about the big picture.

Ask your family if they would prefer an extra vacation every year or for you to come home every day with a smile on your face. While you're at it, ask them if they want new or used underwear. I think you know the answer to both.

So, provided you're not trying to escape from your chosen profession, then your task is very simple. You have your entire time off to conduct your search for a new job. At whatever time you deem appropriate for your industry and position (maybe six months in?), start looking for a new job. This time, focus on finding a position you will love.

If your prospective employer is curious why you aren't currently working, your Year Off Journal will contain all the answers you need. Tell them about the habits and skills you are building to ensure that your next job/career is for the long term. Tell them how you managed your finances responsibly, planned carefully, and took this time off. Tell them about your volunteer work, family reconnecting, and good-doing. All these details should look fantastic to your next boss. Your YO Journal will also contain valuable information about what you are or are not willing to accept in a new job. You can even try to negotiate a sabbatical every five years!

Take your time, consult your circle of trusted advisors, and find a job that matches your life and personality and allows you to grow. Now that's living!

Change Careers

Many are the reasons we find ourselves in a job we can't stand, with people we can't stomach. And those reasons aren't particularly important: how you got here is now out of your control. Staying, however, is 100 percent in your control, and nobody else is going to fix this problem for you.

It is increasingly common to enjoy several different occupations in your lifetime. Your year off may be enough time to train for a new profession, but you need to start thinking about it now. The exercises in this chapter and others will help you narrow your focus before you begin your time off. For example, if you vow never to work weekends again, then becoming a firefighter isn't the answer for you.

If you know the time has come for a complete change in your career field, how do you go about it? If you know the direction you want to go in, you can focus your prep time leading up to your break on setting you up for success in your new profession. You can work on networking and informational interviewing in your target field. You might test-drive some part-time or volunteer work or start exploring that genius business idea you've been sitting on for a while. Finding an entirely new career is a process that needs to be worked at methodically until you find the answer.

A career change can be terrifying if you allow what you do to become a representation of who you are, but you are so much more than your occupation. Don't let it dictate how you spend the rest of the limited time you have.

When to Mention Your Year Off

Whether you hope to take a yearlong sabbatical with your company's blessing, find a different job in your industry, or change careers, you will eventually face the same decision: when should I bring this up with my employer?

At my firm, my employees could have this conversation with me the moment it entered their mind without being concerned about their paycheck or my attitude while they sorted everything out. That said, my advice to anyone who doesn't work for me is this: don't tell your boss until you have to.

Why the conflicting advice? Your boss didn't write a book called *The Year Off*. As great as your boss may be, at the end of the day, everybody has to cover their backside. There is a decent chance that when you tell your boss your plans, you will be looked at as someone who "isn't committed" to the company, whatever the hell that means.

Here is my rationale. I want *you* setting the start date of your year off, not your pissed-off boss kick-starting it with a pink slip. Show your company and your boss the appropriate amount of respect, with the appropriate amount of notice, but don't invite trouble by letting them in too early.

You might be tempted to tell your coworkers about your plans first. You may even want to ask them for advice, since they know your company and your boss as well as you do. Don't do it. Chad in Human Resources may be great company at a happy hour, but that doesn't mean spreading a little office gossip about you wouldn't spice up his day.

The company that has been signing your paychecks deserves respect, and so do you. Work with your accountability partner to make decisions, tap your circle of trust for advice, and don't give your employer a reason to replace you until you have to.

Bringing Friends and Family on Board

If you thought your boss was tough to negotiate with, you haven't seen anything yet. People depend on you, and very few enjoy change. Your spouse, kids, parents, and even neighbors may all rely on you to a certain degree. The people and connections affected by your plans could be virtually limitless.

Most of your circle is going to be behind you all the way, while some of your circle will be weirdos who don't know how to react. The one thing they all have in common, however, is that their initial reaction will include some degree of wondering, "How does this affect me?" Each tier of people in your life will require its own strategy for getting them excited to support your plans.

Immediate Household: Your Circle of Trust

At my house, when I am excited about something, I ask my spouse to read an article or a chapter of a book I am enjoying. It then stays open on the counter for three weeks until it's covered up by the kids' homework and Cheetos. At this point I admit defeat, take my book back and sulk in the corner.

What this has taught me over the years is that my spouse is dealing with her own stuff. Your partner wants to support you, but they are still human. They may not want to read this book or be your accountability partner (as you probably discovered). And that's okay. Spouses are here to support you and also to keep you grounded.

Start the conversation in your household by focusing on the *why* that you developed at the beginning of this chapter. Don't put your family in a difficult position of having to immediately react to your saying you don't want to work for a year. What do you think they are going to say? They don't want to work for a year either! Or do work around the house. Or take crap from the kids.

(And speaking of kids, here's a quick note about children who may be living with you, no matter what age they are: They're kids. They work for you, not the other way around. You don't need their permission!)

Besides possibly being jealous, those closest to you will most likely be worried about you holding up your end of the household responsibilities, including the money part. Reassure them that you will not do anything foolish—you're following the Year Off Money System. Discuss the habits you are developing to make both your life and your household more sustainable over the long run. Outline how your plans give you the flexibility to make the changes you want. Center the conversation around how this time off will ultimately give your family more security in the long run.

Have an open and honest discussion with your partner about why you want to do this and how it will benefit both of you. And when you do, be open to the fact that you may not be the only person in your house in search of something more. (Maybe your loved one *does* want to read this book!)

Friends and Extended Family: Choose Wisely

Those pictures of your friends sitting on a gorgeous Hawaii beach don't make you too jealous, because you went to the Caribbean last year. When your cousin tells you about Jakey winning his Little League tournament, you can be happy for them, because your kid just made honor roll. And when your friend tells you how they are organizing their life so they can take a full year off of work, you will be happy for them because . . . wait, WTF? A whole *year*?

When you tell your friends and close family members about your plans to play hooky for a year, their typical first thought will be jealousy. Your friends may be excited for you on the outside, but they might need some adjustment time. (Why you? *They* work harder, deal with more crap, and deserve it more than you do . . .)

But it's not their fault, and they still love you. When we react to something new and different, our first thoughts are not always our proudest moments. I am constantly fighting my animal instincts to compete with others or want something that someone else has. Millions of years of evolution urging you to advance the fastest can be a tough instinct to overcome.

Over the intermediate to long term, your friends will be supportive and caring and want you to succeed. Bring them in on your plans, and bring them in soon, but here is my advice: bring them in a little piece at a time. Here are the phases:

1. Tell them you have implemented a new money system that is working really well for you and puts you in control of your finances.

2. As you get your money system working, tell them your new money system might give you some freedom to take some time away from work to do something extraordinary and different.

3. As you start to accelerate toward your date, share more of your plans as they shape up, and start to ask for input and help.

You are eventually going to need the support and wisdom of your friends, but let them in a piece at a time. Don't give anyone, not even your best friend, an opportunity to shoot down your plans before you even know what they are. Don't tell them about your destination; invite them into your journey.

Acquaintances: Nah

If you don't get the reaction you were hoping for from your spouse, friends, and family, it's natural to keep moving farther from your inner circle to get that response. Don't do this.

It may feel great that the UPS driver "gets" you in a way that your sister doesn't, but don't be that person. Sign for your damn package and move on with your day. You haven't taken on this process to impress people you barely know or show off on social media. Taking a year off is about finding a greater purpose for your life (at which point you will, hopefully, no longer feel the urge to impress people you barely know).

You probably don't have to think too far back to recall a time when you confided in someone and didn't get the reaction or support you were hoping for. This experience is more common than not, because we tend to build up enormous expectations about what we expect from others in reaction to what we are doing. Remember that your circle won't see things the same way you do. They have different experiences, desires, and troubles of their own to deal with. This doesn't mean they don't care; it simply means they can't see what you see. Yet.

Roadblocks you'll encounter along the way to your year off will include relationship trouble, issues with friends, and problems at work. Life will happen; it always does. You may be tempted to look at the "stuff" thrown your way as obstacles keeping you from your goal. Don't.

Anchor yourself in the big picture. Experiment with setting up strong habits and see how well you can get those working. You want to take time off, yes, but more importantly, you want to be a person who is disciplined enough to do it. Start talking to loved ones who you know will support you, and keep moving forward to find meaning and purpose in your life.

Chapter 6 Accountability
CHECKLIST

Check Your Why

1. Complete the Record Your Wants and Don't Wants exercise to list the things you don't want to deal with in your year off as well as things you want to incorporate into that time.

2. Complete the List Your Regrets exercise to build a road map for how to live a satisfying life.

Build Strong Habits

3. Start a morning routine that includes a written schedule with at least five items.

4. Start a Year Off Journal, and set a regular time daily or weekly to record your thoughts.

5. Start a to-do list that you actively use every day.

Plan Your Time Off From Your Job

6. Discuss your options for leaving your current employment with your accountability partner—and don't tell your boss you're leaving until it's time.

Build Your Circle of Trust

7. Break the news to your immediate household.

8. Break the news to your friends.

9. Break the news to your extended family.

Accountability Partner

Share your morning routine, journaling plans, and to-do list ideas with your AP. Try it for a week and check in with your partner about your success.

CHAPTER 7

Accelerating Your YO System

"Four years! What's the point of even trying?" Nikki slumped back in her chair after seeing her year off date for the first time. "It might as well be fifty years. I thought we were going to figure out how to do this *soon*."

Apparently, she thought my title was Financial Magician, not Financial Planner.

I understand the frustration. When you start to clearly see the direction you want to move your life in, you don't want to wait. It's like eagerly anticipating a road trip, spending hours preparing and packing and jumping into your car, overflowing with excitement. And then there is a traffic jam in your driveway.

As your long-term vision starts to gain clarity, short-term obstacles seem to materialize out of nowhere. This will always be the catch-22 of moving your life toward something that matters.

When you aren't going anywhere, nothing is in your way. Obstacles started appearing for Nikki that day, the day she could first feel how desperately she wanted to commit herself to finding more meaning. We had calculated that her year off date was four years away, but I assured her she would be getting there much sooner than anticipated.

More importantly, it was essential for her to realize the process had already begun.

The starting line isn't the day you leave your job; it's the first day you decide to understand where your money is going. And as I showed Nikki—and as I'm about to show you—you have more control over your year off timeline than you might think.

My client wanted her time off to start *now*, and I didn't blame her. I explained to her that everyone's year off starts at the same time: when they are ready. The good news is your readiness isn't out of your control; both the monetary side and the intention side are something you can improve every day. The tips in this chapter for accelerating your year off date will financially prepare you for your time off. More importantly, they will help prepare you mentally as well.

In Chapter 5, you calculated your number of months until your time off. I gave you a few hints for moving your money to the right: out of your overhead costs and toward freedom. I also told you that if you didn't like what you saw when you did those calculations, I'd show you how to shrink the time until your year off date by putting your money to work for you.

In this chapter, we will focus on more strategies for shaving months or even years off your year off date.

Moving Your Money Right

With all its buckets and accounts, the Year Off Money System is all about moving your money to the right, from today's bills toward Future You.

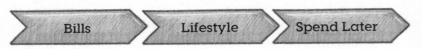

Your goal in this chapter is simple: find every way you can to slide your money to the right. Now is the time to start weighing your priorities, like: which is more important to you, a year working for

Habitat for Humanity and fixing your relationships, or buying new kayaks next week that will sit in your garage three out of four weekends? Your options are simple:

1. Reduce your personal overhead so you can have more money to spend during your time away from your job.
2. Reduce your lifestyle spending so you can build up your Year Off Accounts, and so your lifestyle isn't dependent on your job.
3. Focus on growing your Year Off Account.

Wherever you are today—whatever the numbers you put together in Chapter 3 show—if you want your year off date to move closer, start moving your money to the right.

At this point, the money flowing out of your bank account might look something like this:

Overhead Bucket	Lifestyle Bucket	Spend Later (Year Off) Bucket
Mortgage: $1,600	Monthly Transfer 1: $1,500	Spend Soon Account: $500
Utilities: $200		
Car Payment: $300	Monthly Transfer 2: $1,500	Roth IRA: $250
Internet/TV: $100		
Auto Insurance: $150		
Student Loan: $100		
Other Debt: $500		
Cell Phone: $100		
Gym Membership: $50		

In the example above, Nikki's initial year off date was forty-eight months away. If you're facing a similar timeline, while it may feel like a lifetime, remember: that number is completely within your control. Let's look at three main ways you can accelerate your timeline and put your money to work for you.

Fewer Bills, More Life

Nobody sets out to acquire bills. You don't enter a new year thinking, "Hey, it's time to add more permanent overhead to my life so I can limit my freedom and chain myself to my job!" Excessive overhead expenses don't happen all at once. We add them piece by piece as life happens around us.

- You want to fix up the house, so you open a home equity line of credit and do a few projects. Since you have that credit line, you might as well do a couple of other projects too, and the payment increases.
- Then your car crosses the 125,000-mile mark and starts to have trouble. What's another $350 a month for a car payment? You can handle that.
- Meanwhile, you forgot to pay off the new living room furniture you put on the credit card to get the miles—oops.
- Surprise! One of the kids needs braces. That also goes on the credit card, swelling the monthly payment.

You get the idea. If you don't stay laser-focused on your overhead, it will increase. Now is the time to look at where you are and start reducing your bills. No judgment—you likely had good reasons. But now it's time to move forward.

Why Cutting Bills Has a Double Effect

How are you able to accelerate your year off date so rapidly with only small- to moderate-sized changes in your life? The reason is almost too simple: Every change you make impacts both sides of the equation. It's a double whammy. When you permanently eliminate a regular living expense and redirect that money toward your Year Off Account, you are not only reducing your overhead on one side but also increasing your savings by the same amount.

Think about it. If Nikki eliminates a $500 monthly debt payment, the money she needs to live on each month is reduced by $500. Now she doesn't need to save as much for her year off. Not only that, she now has an extra $500 to put away for later. This is not a monthly swing of $500 in your plan—it's a change of $1,000! You get to double your pleasure and double your fun with every dollar you cut from your budget!

Now, let's look at two places where it is fairly easy to get your money back—paying down debt and cutting unnecessary expenses—and look a little more closely at why trimming your monthly bills works so well to accelerate your year off date and improve your ease of living.

Example 1: Reduce Your Debt (and Payments)

In our sample spending above, you can see $500 per month is going toward paying down consumer debt, which includes loans for things like vehicles, furniture, boats, and whatever else you put on the credit card. To reduce your monthly expenses, simply find ways to pay down or pay off these balances (and then don't increase them again), and pay off the highest-interest loans first. No balance, no payment!

Let's say that through a series of extra payments and selling some old household items to pay off your debt, you are able to eliminate those payments. Now, an extra $500 per month has been freed up to go into your Year Off Account, which will build up faster.

	Old YO Plan	New YO Plan (after deleting $500 in monthly payments)
Annual Spending	$72,000	$66,000
Monthly YO Account	$500	$1,000

This change would accelerate your year off date by 78 months, or almost 50%.

Example 2: Whittle Down Your Optional Monthly Bills

In my experience, most people can find $50 a month in bills they can save almost instantly. If wiping out $500 worth of debt payments seemed a little ambitious in the first example, look at what eliminating even one minor expense can do for you. For example, let's say you realize that you spend all your time on Netflix and don't need your premium channel cable subscription anymore, so you cancel it and save about $50 a month.

Even this minor savings of $50 a month will help more than you think. In this case, eliminating $50 from your budget moves your year off date up almost fourteen full months!

	Old YO Plan	New YO Plan (after deleting $50 in monthly payments)
Annual Spending	$72,000	$71,600
Monthly YO Account	$500	$550
This change would accelerate your year off date by 14 months.		

These numbers can feel so far away, but we have almost unlimited control to change them and make taking a year off a reality as soon as we want.

Less Lifestyle Creep, More Freedom

Looking at our bills, it is easy to put them in the context of monthly payments. An extra $500 monthly payment is not a hard concept to grasp. It will cost $500/month, every month, until it stops. With lifestyle spending, it's very different. Lifestyle expenses are a long series of one-offs. When we increase our lifestyle spending, it doesn't feel like a permanent increase in our spending. The problem occurs when it becomes permanent.

For example, splurging on a nicer hotel, bigger rental car, and expensive wining and dining for your summer vacation doesn't feel like you are permanently taking on more expense. After all, a vacation is a onetime event and if you have the money then you have the money. The problem arrives the following year when it's time to book your vacation. Are you really going back to the garden view room with two queens after you experienced the oceanfront room with a king bed and softer robes?

Or an interior room? Of course not, this isn't medieval times. You work hard for your money and want to treat yourself right.

Lifestyle creep is real. It starts in college when you switch from canned to bottled beer and never go back. When you get your first car with heated seats and anything less feels uncivilized. What ends up in your shopping cart these days, chuck steak or the brisket?

Slow and steady changes to your lifestyle (always upward) is the reason that a separate checking account is necessary for your lifestyle purchases. Unless you are uber-intentional or a penny-pincher about where your money goes, it will go to pamper Current You. And the sad thing is, you won't even notice.

Instead of letting your money slip through your fingers like this, let's look at what aspects may not be necessary, and get your money moving to the right.

Example 1: Delay the Home Improvements

Everyone likes to pick on eating out as the place they spend too much money, and that may be true, but I think the easiest target is household spending. This is the amount of money you spend on a regular basis to improve your living situation.

My wife is an interior designer, so I want to tread lightly here, but doesn't your house look good how it is now? In this category, your expenses are based 100 percent on your opinions and your choices. Would you rather have your current, perfectly functional house and a nice long break from work, or a new kitchen or couch that you don't see from nine to five every day?

It may seem like the money you spend on your house is under control, but I find most people don't have a sense of it. Have a look through your bank statements. Add up the spending at Ross, TJ Maxx, Target, and yes, even Amazon. I'm guessing that it isn't a small amount of money.

Spending money on your home isn't bad. The problem is that, until now, it has gone unprioritized. You didn't have this new dream to put first. If you decide moving up your year off date is more important than new pillows for your couch, look at what reducing your lifestyle expenses by $250 a month (or $3,000 a year) can do:

	Old YO Plan	New YO Plan (after eliminating your $250 pillow habit)
Annual Spending	$72,000	$69,000
Monthly YO Account	$500	$750
This change would accelerate your year off date by 52 months.		

Example 2: Reconsider Your Travel Options

I pick on travel a lot as a category where too much money is spent, but I am guilty of excessive travel myself. I live in the northern part of the country where winters are cold and annoying. Rarely does a February go by where I don't spend a little too much money to go somewhere warm for a week.

You may be the type to take tropical vacations, or maybe you're the active type who sticks to camping trips near your house. Regardless, almost anyone can save a little bit of money by paying attention to how they travel: skip the room upgrade, prepare more meals in advance, or don't buy a new tent when your existing one still has four walls and a mostly functional roof.

If you can find a way to cut back on your travel by even $100 a month on average ($1,200 a year), which I find most people can, you can still see significant savings.

	Old YO Plan	New YO Plan (after shaving $100 in monthly travel)
Annual Spending	$72,000	$70,800
Monthly YO Account	$500	$600
This change would accelerate your year off date by 26 months.		

As you can see, reducing your monthly transfer to your Lifestyle Account by $100 will move up your year off date by 26 months. Isn't that worth sacrificing your ocean view every once in a while?

Example 3: Quit Swimming in the World's Biggest River

Holy crap, people, how much money are we going to spend at Amazon? The answer is more than last year, apparently. Online spending is something I personally have to keep an eye on or it can get out of control quickly.

My online spending seems to be directly related to my general crankiness: the less I want to be around people in public stores, the more I buy everything I need online. My last four orders from Amazon are garden hose, shower head, butter, and shoes. Those items don't seem unreasonable do they? I use the shoes daily and the shower head weekly.

The issue with your Amazon account—or any other online retailer you have grown accustomed to—is it's too easy to use. If you are like me, you go from thought in your head about what you need to receiving an order confirmation in about thirty seconds.

When we are on autopilot with our online purchases, we aren't evaluating how necessary the item we just ordered is. We click "Buy Now" before we even think about what it's costing us. Do I need that home water testing kit because I think my neighbors are poisoning me, or do I need to keep my lifestyle spending in check so I can steadily decrease my number of months until freedom?

Whatever you can save, do the math for yourself and watch your months drop away.

Greater Focus on Your Year Off Account

Your steady paycheck likely isn't the only money that is deposited into your bank account throughout the year. You might sell a few household items, do some extra work for cash, receive a cash gift from a family member, or even get a bonus at work. If you are not paying close attention, this money will enter your checking account and slowly be whittled away until you have nothing to show for it (that you can remember, anyway . . . it must have gone somewhere).

Putting aside your found money can have a dramatic impact on accelerating your YO System timeline. Make a commitment in advance: any money I receive outside of my regular paycheck will go directly into my Year Off Account, not my Lifestyle Account. Buying something extra or "treating myself" is not an option. Your *year off* is your new big treat (and no calories!).

Example 1: Repurpose Your Tax Refund

According to the IRS, the average taxpayer receives a refund of about $2,800. Most of my clients treat it like free money, like it dropped in out of the sky. They spend that money on luxury items, impulsive splurges, and other things they don't need.

But you know what? The money in that check is money you *earned*. You sent too much to the IRS over the year, and now they are sending it back. It's not free money. You worked for it. What if you took that money and put it in your Year Off Account before you found a place to spend it?

	Old YO Plan	New YO Plan
Annual Spending	$72,000	$72,000
Monthly YO Account	$500	$500
Even though your bucket amounts haven't changed, putting the refund in your YO Account will move your year off date 6 months closer.		

Putting aside an average tax return amount will get you to your year of freedom nearly six months sooner. Doing this for two years in a row shaves off an entire year. If you want to treat it like "free money" that came from nowhere, give it to Future You without breaking a sweat. Focusing on the little things can add up big time.

Example 2: Start a Side Hustle

Everybody do the hustle—the side hustle, that is. Making a little extra coin on the side is now easier than ever. It used to be that if you wanted part-time income you had to get a part-time job. This meant getting an application, having an interview, and watching grainy training videos from the eighties.

Not anymore. Now that this whole internet thing is looking like the real deal, you don't even need to leave your house to make a little extra money. You can make an extra $100 a month. Anyone can make an extra $100 a month.

Setting aside that much extra money into your Year Off Account will accelerate your year off date by five months. And if you find a way to make extra money every month, you might have months where you make several hundred.

	Old YO Plan	New YO Plan (after deleting $50 in monthly payments)
Annual Spending	$72,000	$72,000
Monthly YO Account	$500	$600
This additional income would accelerate your year off date by 24 months, or two years!		

Working yourself to the bone to move up your year off date, however, isn't a good idea. We are looking for a way to add more purpose and less stress to your life. Adding more hours to your day isn't something that is going to help.

What will help is looking around you for opportunity. If you can find a way to make a little extra money that doesn't stress you out, do it. Commit in advance to setting that money aside so you can continue to move your year off date as close as possible.

Both of those examples above are extremely doable. I hope this section gave you ideas for how to free up some of your money in your life. Most of my clients find areas within their bills, lifestyle, and miscellaneous income where they can make change. All it takes is a commitment to pay attention.

If you calculated a high number of months in Chapter 5, don't worry. Each of the strategies listed above will shorten your wait until your year off, and they're even more powerful when you can combine multiple strategies together. Imagine if you could do just three of the examples I listed above, one in each category. Wiping out a chunk of debt could potentially lower your overhead $500 per month. Monitoring the amount of money you spend on your home could reduce your lifestyle spending by $250. And setting aside your tax refund every year could put nearly $3,000 in your YO Account.

Add those together, and you have shortened your wait time by a combined ninety-six months, or eight years! You can overcome any obstacles that are now in your way; you just need a system.

Find Your Own Shortcuts

The examples above are only that: examples. The details may not be relevant to your unique situation, but that doesn't mean you can't find your own ways to move your money to the right.

Recently I found my son's math test on the counter with a red "9/10" marked at the top. Very good, I thought, but I couldn't help scanning the page to locate the offending question. After adding up all the pigs, cows, and ducks on the farm for myself, I got the same answer he did. What was going on?

In the margin was a big red X with the words "show your work" next to it. Now, that triggered a few issues for me and I quickly changed his 9/10 to 10/10 and showed it to him. "You didn't get the question wrong, buddy," I told him. "You got it right, and you shouldn't be penalized because you can get the answers right away."

We seem to be teaching our kids from their earliest days that finding your own answers, figuring out the best way for them to work, is not a positive attribute. Luckily for you, school is out. Shortcuts are awesome, and I encourage you to find as many (legal ones) as you can. Never mind being penalized. Looking for shortcuts to your destination can help you think outside the box and crawl out of the rut you've been stuck in. If you can accomplish a task faster, go for it. What that teacher thought of as a "shortcut," I call "the process."

With that in mind—and with the previous examples to get you started—I challenge you to find all the shortcuts you can to accelerate the system and move up your year off date.

Putting Your Year Off Money to Work

If you thought discussing budgets was fun, then strap in, because we are switching topics to investing! Don't skip the rest of this chapter though; we are only skimming the surface. I won't put you through a detailed conversation on one of the most boring topics in the world, but I do think it's important to give you an overview of your options.

Too many Investment Advisors like to bore you with details of the stock market, interest rates, and asset allocation. Often their goal isn't even to educate you—it's to make themselves look smart. Since you already know I can add up farm animals all by myself, we're going to look at investments with a different goal in mind: finding simple ones that will accelerate your year off date.

Where Should I Set Up My Year Off Account?

This is one of the first questions I get after I help a client get the YO System up and running. Back in Chapter 4, we walked through the steps for setting up your Year Off Account in a checking account, and that works well for many people. However, you have a few options for storing this money as you contribute to it: a savings account, money market, savings apps on your phone. But putting that money to work for you by investing it wisely could shave months off your wait time.

Investing can feel intimidating to some, but coordinating your accounts can lead to a significant acceleration in building up your Year Off Account. Let's look at one example to see how wise investing can help you reach those goals sooner.

In the table below, we will consider the difference between earning nothing on your money and earning 5 percent.

Current YO Account Balance	Monthly Savings Over Five Years	Interest Rate	Balance
$18,000	$500	0%	$48,000
$18,000	$500	5%	$57,245

In the scenario above, you would have accomplished two very important things. First, by earning interest, you have cut months off your year off date by earning an extra $9,000. That isn't chump change. Second, you will have established a lifelong habit of investing your excess money. As your assets grow, this can lead to tens of thousands of dollars that *you*, not the bank, will earn over your lifetime. And what could be more satisfying than legally taking money from a bank?

Investing your money is part of spending intentionally. It may feel like a hassle at first—or even like you are being greedy by wanting every last penny—but that isn't true. You are simply developing the habits that will allow you to maximize the resources available for your time off.

There is additional interest to be earned on your money beyond what the bank is offering you. Either you can have it, or the bank can have it. Personally, I would rather you have it, because I suspect that you will put it to better use than a shady Wall Street bank.

Year Off Date: 0–12 Months Away

Rousing anti-bank speech aside, if your year off date is less than twelve months away, just keep your money in the damn bank. If you get too creative with your investments, your Year Off Account value can drop right when you need the money. If you have less than a year to go, it isn't worth risking it going down a couple of percentage points, and the interest you'll make over the next year or less won't be enough to make a drastic impact.

I may be no fan of banks, but for short-term money, they are still the place to be. Drop your cash in a money market account at your local credit union and be done with it.

Year Off Date: 12–36 Months Away

If you are more than a year away from your time off, then putting your money to work in a fairly tame investment will make the most sense for you. Yes, your balance will go up and down a bit. Yes, that's okay.

If your break from work falls within this time frame, you will want to open a taxable (non-retirement) investment account with an investment company. You can open an account online yourself or work with a financial planner (more on that later).

What you are looking for is a "conservative" or "capital preservation" portfolio. Investments like these will invest in mostly bonds, with a few stocks, and should average around 4 percent returns annually. Your exact returns will vary year to year, but you will be better off overall for making the investment.

Year Off Date: 36+ Months Away

The farther away your year off, the more aggressively you can invest your money. *Aggressive* is a relative term, however. Your Future You (retirement) accounts should be invested aggressively, especially if you have a decade or two ahead of you, but don't go too crazy with your Year Off Account.

If you are more than three years away from your time off, invest your Year Off Account in a "balanced" or "moderate" portfolio. Your balance will go up and down on a regular basis, but as long as you are contributing to the account monthly, you should come out significantly ahead in the end. Regular contributions are the key strategy here, the system that makes this work. When the market goes down, your contribution will buy more at a lower price. When it goes up, hey, presto—your money is worth more.

Don't be afraid of putting your money to work for you. Ups and downs are a natural part of money management and of life. Look at the big picture, and know that investing patiently will pay dividends (literally) over the long run. And that will move your time off even closer.

Keeping It All Together

Putting money front and center in your life may feel strange. You may have heard the saying, "Money is the root of all evil." So shouldn't you show that you have no interest in evil things by completely ignoring money? Unfortunately, that isn't how this journey works. We can't ignore the issues that wreak havoc in our lives; we have to master them. Or at least get them under control. Money is your ticket. You can fight it, but you will only slow your own progress.

Now that you have your bank accounts open, your investments account established, and your monthly contributions set up, you can cruise on autopilot, right? Hardly. The hard work may be done, but keeping your money system running smoothly will require continuous attention and maintenance. Nothing worth doing in life is "set it and forget it," and your money is no different.

There is a saying in business that "what gets measured gets improved." This means that unless you are paying attention, your system will stagnate. With the YO System, we have opted out of setting up an elaborate budgeting system, where you have to look at your finances daily. But you still have to actively keep things on track.

Here are a few easy steps you can implement right away.

Set Up Automated Reminders

Unless you are at a super old-school bank, you probably have the option to set up automated alerts on your account. For example, you can set balance thresholds for your bank account which will trigger alerts. My preferred method of alert is to receive a text message. I have them set on my checking accounts to get notified when my balance hits $500, $250, and $100. It helps me tighten my belt on spending toward the end of the month.

Your credit card should have a similar feature. Some of you (myself included) can't give up the airline miles yet and are incorporating a credit card into your system. While there is nothing wrong with that, you have to stay vigilant. Set up your credit alerts for a certain level (e.g., $1,000, $2,000) so you always have enough money in your Lifestyle Account to pay the entire bill each month.

Stick to the System

While most personal finance books, worksheets, and blogs make it feel as if sitting down and creating a line-by-line budget of every dollar you spend is the only responsible path to adulting, in reality, budgets are hard to come up with and even harder to stick to.

Technology was supposed to solve this problem for us. Popular online budgeting tools are intended to automate the process of tracking your spending down to the last penny. Rather than simplify our lives, however, these tools have become one more website or app you are too busy to monitor and end up not caring about.

Why doesn't it work? Life—and your spending—varies drastically each month. You don't spend $250 eating out every month, you spend $149.88 one month and $423.16 the next. You spend 50 percent more money in December and pay 20 percent more the month your car insurance bill arrives. You buy $600 of clothes one month and a pair of socks the next.

But when your budgeting system breaks and you give up, your brain files the whole thing away as a bad experience, and you swear you will never try budgeting again. From there, you manage your finances by glancing at your checking account balance every week or so. Or by whipping out plastic and figuring it out in the perpetual "later."

Although you may be paying your bills on time, when you wing it, you are not actually getting ahead. You are simply treading water while your money disappears. The hard truth is this: to take a long-term break, you need a system. The process in this book is pretty simple when you take it in small bites. You just have to keep chewing.

I have learned that the key to getting closer is simple: keep moving. Imagine climbing into your vehicle in your driveway without starting the engine. Are you going to see anything cool or do anything awesome? Of course not. You can't steer a parked car! To dominate your time off, you need to keep the system running, and that means doing a little bit toward your Year Off Money System each day.

Without a system in place to keep you on track with your spending, you will never be building your destiny, only repairing what barely works already. Without sticking to that system, you won't be moving toward something bigger, simply rearranging the dining chairs on the Hindenburg.

Hire a Professional

You can always hire a financial planner, accountant, or other coach to hold you accountable to your goals, especially if you've had trouble managing your money well in the past. Find someone that you aren't going to give fake answers to. (Yes, doctor, I only drink "socially.") To help you avoid the armpits of this industry, I have a bit more to say about this in the next chapter.

Accountability isn't a goal; it's a habit that you can develop. When you start building and refining a routine that forces you to look at the reality of your situation, not the fantasy version in your head, Future You will thank you. Then, when times get tough, you will have a system you can depend on when life starts to pull you off course.

Keep Checking In With Your Accountability Partner

People want to help you. Sometimes they want to help you before you even ask for it, but their intentions are usually pure. Make sure you set up a regular check-in with your accountability partner. If it's your spouse, find a time of the week where you always review your money system and how things are going, even if you just spend five minutes on it. My time is Sunday night; that is when I get everything organized for the next week and make sure I am on the same money page with my wife.

If it's a friend, a standing lunch or coffee date works well. The first Thursday of every month, the fifteenth of every month—what matters is sticking to it. Pick your best time and schedule the dates on your calendar system for the next twelve months so you don't get all weird and start ignoring the person who is going to hold you accountable.

Chapter 7 Accountability
CHECKLIST

Less Overhead and More Life

1. Go through your bills and credit card statements and look for opportunities to reduce or eliminate expenses that are currently in your bills account. Make the phone calls and adjust your year off date!

Less Lifestyle Creep and More Freedom

2. Take a look at your Lifestyle Account for areas where you can cut back on your spending without drastically altering your lifestyle. Move this money to your Year Off Account to accelerate your timeline.

More Focus on your Year Off Account

3. Repurpose your tax refund, start a side hustle, or find your own shortcuts to shave months off your wait.

Put Your Year Off Account to Work

4. If your year off date is more than twelve months away look for an investment solution to put your money to work. More resources on finding an investment solution can be found at RightMoney.com.

5. Set up automated balance alerts through your bank and credit card company to hold you accountable

Accountability Partner

6. Plan regular check-ins with your accountability partner for this chapter. Schedule them out for the next year, right now!

CHAPTER 8

Settling Your Affairs and Saying Goodbye

Jill wanted to spend her year off traveling and made no apologies for it. She could tell I was winding up for a lecture about spending valuable time bumming around like a college student, and she had her defense prepared well in advance. She wasn't going to spend a year sitting on a beach sipping mai tais (although even I have to admit a few weeks of that wouldn't kill anyone). She had a specific plan in mind.

First of all, Jill wanted to discover where she wanted to live next. She had been in the same house for about five years. She had friends around, but not much family. "Do I really like this town and this house," she wondered, "or am I just here because of inertia?"

The second reason for traveling was to spend time on relationships she had let lapse. It's a lot easier to ask an old friend to stay with you for a week in Paris than it is to ask them to set up shop in your extra bedroom in the—yawn—suburbs for an extended visit.

Her final motivation for traveling was work-related. Already a remote employee in the job that she was planning to leave, Jill wanted to take it up a step and work remotely from all over the world by starting her own consulting business. If Jill could work while traveling, she could work anywhere once she returned. Other goals included expanding her potential client base outside of the United States and seeing what specific problems needed to be solved in other parts of the world.

She had done a great job of working the Year Off Money System and was right on the cusp of leaving her job. When it came to her safety net, however, she always had an excuse for not dealing with it. But now that she was taking the trip of a lifetime, she couldn't ignore it any longer.

Building a safety net isn't just for those who plan to travel. When your year begins and your life starts to evolve rapidly, you really won't want to deal with the "boring" details you've been neglecting. Everyone undergoing major life changes will need to sort out their safety nets and get their affairs in order. Especially with a year away from your job, from where so much of your safety net comes—health care, life insurance, and disability insurance, to name a few—there are loose ends you need to tie up *before* you go.

Many of my clients in their sixties still feel like legal documents and insurance are for the generation above them to worry about, but I can assure you this is not the case. Life can turn upside-down in an instant. Every year, I see the financial wreckage left behind by a spouse or parent that was too proud, lazy, or scared to address their legal and insurance issues.

Many of us have trained ourselves to block out negativity and focus only on the positive, so making room in your mind for your own mortality is not something that happens often. Boring legal and insurance crap is never high on the to-do list.

Well, I have good news and bad news for you. The bad news is your eventual death is a near certainty, and you have no idea when that day is coming. If you want to enjoy a responsible break from work and take care of your family (or future family), you need to join reality and get your affairs in order. This includes a plan for dealing with your insurance (including health care) and legal documents should something happen to you.

This might be painful and boring to think about, but here's the good news: *once you do it, you are set for a long time.* I'm not going to lie and say it's completely "set it and forget it," but it's pretty close. You won't have to look at these items again until many years have gone by or you experience a major life change.

In this chapter, I will do my best to help you check off these necessary boxes quickly and painlessly so that you are prepared for the unexpected, whether during your year off or in the future.

Setting Up Your Safety Net

Let's deal with the elephant in the book right now. When you step away from your job, you will likely lose your health insurance, some form of life insurance, and more—your health safety net. We both know that you could have picked up any of the thousands of books on personal finance that try to teach you about those things by now. You didn't, because you don't want to learn how to be a bean-counter. You want to take time off to pursue your dreams and build a better life.

I'm not going to teach you any new concepts in this section. Instead, I will provide checklists for things you might need to consider. Use them to finish building your safety net ahead of embarking on your journey!

Health Insurance

With less stress and more freedom, a year away may even improve your health, but that doesn't mean you don't need a good health insurance plan! Accidents happen, and they can be expensive. Health insurance is a complex topic, and it doesn't seem to be getting any easier to manage. However, taking a long break from your job sometimes means upsetting your current health care situation.

Here are a few items to consider to keep your health care on track while making major changes in your life.

- Your health insurance may currently be provided by your employer. No job, no health insurance! Start to research and understand the individual health insurance marketplace if that is where you will have to go for a solution.

- You may be eligible for COBRA through your job. This means you can stay on your current health plan (at full price) after you leave your job for 18 months. This is a great backup plan, but should not be your primary strategy (trust me, talk to someone about it).
- Since you'll be experiencing a drastic reduction in income, you may be eligible for a subsidy on your health insurance, making the whole exercise much more affordable.
- If you are traveling out of state or out of country during your year off, different health plans will have different rules. Make sure you look at the out-of-area coverage offered if you plan on being mobile during your time off, and look into traveler's medical insurance where appropriate to fill in the gaps.

Remember to calculate your insurance costs into your year off living expenses!

EXERCISE:
Health Insurance Checklist

Make a list now of any open health insurance questions that come to mind, then check them off as you do more research and tie up any loose ends.

- [ ] ....
- [ ] ....
- [ ] ....
- [ ] ....
- [ ] ....

Life Insurance

The best and worst parts of my job often occur at the same moment. Not long ago, a young couple in their early forties, with whom I had been working for several years, came into my office to tell me that the husband had a rare form of lung cancer. Sadly, the doctor had estimated he had less than six months to live. They were scared shitless.

It was a very emotional meeting, but there was only one question on the table that mattered: "Is my wife going to be okay financially after I die?"

She was, but not because of luck. They had been diligent unbudgeters, investors, and YO System savers. He had a decent life insurance policy through work and could purchase a little more even though he was sick. We ran the numbers and thankfully, yes, there would be enough money to get her to retirement and send the kids to college. He would leave a legacy of taking care of his family, with his hard work producing dividends that outlasted both him and his disease.

This stuff is real. You can feel sad when you hear stories about tragedies like this hitting other families, but the real tragedy is being unprepared when it happens to you. Not only will you have to deal with the disease or accident, but bad financial fallout can make your tragedy hurt for years afterward. Real life is coming. You have the power to control what happens next, and you don't have to feel like an idiot.

You may have ignored life insurance your whole life, but now is the time to pay attention. Life insurance is a wonderful thing and worth paying attention to; it's life-insurance *salespeople* you can continue ignoring.

Here are a few things to look at:

- You may have your primary life insurance provided to you as a group life policy through your employer. If you leave your job, no more insurance. Look into getting a policy that you own and is not dependent on your employment.

- Right before your time off, when you have significant savings, you may feel like life insurance is unnecessary. Fast-forward to the end of your time off, when your Year Off Account is running on fumes. You will be glad you already have your life insurance taken care of.
- If you already have insurance double-check your beneficiaries. If something happens to you, your insurance money needs to go to the right place. I have seen insurance proceeds go to a first wife instead of a current wife, and to a sibling instead of to children. This is heartbreaking, don't do that to someone.
- It's not like a term insurance policy is that expensive. Don't be stingy—spend $40 to $50 a month to have your insurance done for the rest of your life.

EXERCISE:
Life Insurance Checklist

Do you have a life insurance policy through your employer? Do you have beneficiaries? Has anything changed in your life since you last checked your life insurance policy? Write down anything you need to check up on, then gather all your information and make any necessary changes.

- [ ] ....
- [ ] ....
- [ ] ....
- [ ] ....
- [ ] ....

I get that you would rather get a hot poker in the eye than deal with insurance or read one more word about it. It's time though. Insurance is one of the necessary evils that isn't fun to deal with, but taking care of it once and for all will be one of your finest moments in adulthood.

Legal Documents

If health insurance didn't provide enough excitement, it's time for legal documents! Getting these in order can be painful. Most people have never hired a lawyer, and tightening up your legal affairs will require the services of one. It may take a little effort, but ask for referrals from your friends and family until you find a starting point.

Your other option is to generate a set of legal documents through an online service or software program. This move is obviously cheaper and more convenient, but if you have any complexities in your life (i.e., you have kids, a previous marriage, or a business), you won't have anyone to work with who can answer the details of your particular situation.

Let's first tackle what documents you need. Please note that what is best for you will be impacted significantly by what state you live in. Any advice in the legal arena needs to be very general to avoid conflicts with your state's particular rules.

1. Living Will and/or Health Care Proxy

You may need one or both of these, depending on your situation. Ask your lawyer. A living will is a document that expresses your preferences for health care treatment should you not be competent (conscious) to make those decisions on your own. The rather large decision of whether to pull the plug on you after your tragic spelunking accident can be made in advance and spelled out in your living will.

A proxy is someone who makes decisions on your behalf, so a health care proxy is someone who has the authority to make health care decisions for you in the event of your incompetence. (This doesn't refer to your general day-to-day incompetency, only your medical incompetency where you are unable to state your preferences.)

2. Durable Power of Attorney

With a durable power of attorney form, you are authorizing someone to make legal and financial decisions on your behalf should you become incapacitated and unable to make decisions for yourself. This document is not only important for a permanent injury, but also a temporary one. It gives someone the opportunity to manage your affairs for a few weeks until you recover.

Remember, this form does not activate until you are unable to make decisions for yourself. Your brother cannot take this form down to the local credit union and clear out your accounts without your permission. Your physical condition typically has to be certified by a court before it becomes active.

3. Will

Hey, finally, one we've all heard of! (As in, "will" you please stop talking about legal documents, Steve?) The will is the most basic and necessary of documents to get done. In its most basic form, this piece of paper determines where your assets go after you die and who is responsible for making sure that happens. The person who ensures that your wishes are carried out according to your will is called an executor.

Let me keep this very simple for you so we can move forward. If you have a reasonably priced attorney to talk to, do it. Odds are you don't, or you would already have your legal docs taken care of. If finding the right person to talk to is holding you back, there are websites where you can get everything taken care of without a lawyer for $150 or so. This online solution can stand in as your backup plan while you search for a local lawyer who is honest and affordable and communicates well. (And after you find this person, you can go hunting for Bigfoot next!)

4. Tech Plan

Society is at a point where technology contingency plans are just as important as life insurance and legal documents. I can't tell you how many times I have watched clients struggle to log in to their 401(k) accounts during a meeting. After a complex sequence of password resets and re-membering their dad's middle name, the street they grew up on, and two-step verifications, they are usually able to log in (but not always).

If you are planning to travel during your time off or work from random coffee shops throughout the week, you need to take your technology plan seriously. The two main areas to pay attention to are passwords and backups.

- **Passwords.** If you are still rocking variations of SpringBreak98@ every time you are prompted for a password, it's time to secure your digital life. I have seen clients pull a folded sheet of paper from their wallet to find an account password. There are better options! It's time to upgrade your piece of paper, spreadsheet (on your computer desktop), or habit of using the same password over and over to have a fighting chance of logging in. Great password managers abound to keep your logins secure.

- **Backups.** With the availability of cloud storage and online backup programs now, you never have an excuse for losing a document again. One trick I started using recently is using a scanning app on my phone. If I have a miscellaneous piece of paper or receipt lying around that I can't bring myself to throw away, I scan and save it to a reference folder in my online storage. Taking advantage of digital systems like this helps me keep my physical life clutter free. All online storage systems do pretty much the same thing, so pick one, set it up, and move on.

Having your technology organized isn't just for you, it's for anyone who may need to help you. If you get stranded overseas or find yourself laid up in a hospital bed, you will need some help. Having all your passwords and documents organized in one place will make life much easier for who-ever cares about you enough to take care of your affairs when you can't.

There—that wasn't so painful, was it?

EXERCISE:
Collect Your Legal Documents

If you don't have all of these documents, take the time now to put them in order. And if you haven't looked at them in a while, make sure the information is up to date.

- [ ] Living will and/or health care proxy
- [ ] Durable power of attorney
- [ ] Will
- [ ] Tech plan

With these checklists in hand, you're on your way to filling in any holes in your safety net and putting all your affair in order so you can take your year off knowing that you've taken the steps to ensure that you or your loved ones are in the best possible position in case of an emergency. And best of all, once those boxes are checked, you won't have to think about any of this again for a very long time.

Using a Professional Advisor: How to Not Get Burned

Two areas where you might consider using a financial professional are monitoring your spending system and investing your Year Off Account into something that will earn a little bit of money for you. If you have a financial advisor that you like and trust already, great. (Well, not so great, actually, because you don't know if they are any good at their job or not. You will find resources at the end of this chapter to help with that particular issue.)

If you discover that you want more help on your journey, smart, caring professionals are out there and available, but you need to know where to look. I recommend a couple of simple guidelines to follow.

Don't Use These People for Financial Advice

Lots of people in your life deal with your money, but that doesn't mean they're the right person to give you advice on what to do with it. Think carefully before asking the following people to help you figure out a financial plan.

- **Your Insurance Agent.** You may think your insurance agent is a financial advisor, but they aren't. Their job is to sell stuff that other people tell them to sell, not to provide advice. Be careful, or you may find your Year Off Account has been transferred to a really expensive life insurance policy.

- **Your CPA.** They are probably kind and honest, but the typical CPA does not specialize in personal financial advice. Your CPA doesn't want to talk about your budget; they want you to refer them a $5,000-per-year corporate tax return.

- **Your Banker.** If you ask a banker where the best place to invest money is, guess what they'll say? The bank. Whatever you are trying to accomplish, they just tell you the bank has a solution for that.

Use a Financial Planner

It may seem like everyone in "finance" does the same thing, but I can assure you nothing could be further from the truth. "Financial advisor" has become the generic term for anyone who is licensed to deal with finance-related products, but you will hear many other terms used as well. A few examples are stockbroker, finance guy, money chick, and dirty insurance salesman.

The primary job of the majority of finance professionals you run into is to sell you something. They can't pay their bills unless they sell you something. You don't want these "advisors" helping you plan for your time off.

One group of advisors doesn't get paid by selling you something: financial planners. They can pay their bills only if they provide you with great advice. Financial planners commit themselves to understanding your objectives, analyzing your resources, and making recommendations that are in your best interests instead of their own.

You will never be certain that someone in finance is acting 100 percent in your best interests, but you can greatly increase the odds by taking a few simple steps. One of those is working with someone who calls themselves a financial planner, not a financial advisor or investment advisor.

There is obviously significantly more detail that goes into finding a financial planner that is right for you. (Maybe someone will write a book about it soon. Oh, wait—*I* did! Look for it online.) In the meantime, you can find more resources on how to find a quality financial planner at yearoff.co.

Chapter 8 Accountability
CHECKLIST

Health Insurance

1. Make a plan for your health insurance. Look at the provisions of your employer coverage to see if staying on COBRA is a viable option for you.

2. Complete the Health Insurance Checklist exercise.

Life Insurance

3. Get an individual insurance policy. If your life insurance is provided through work you need to buy a term insurance policy that you own. Now that you know how much money your family needs per month, calculating the amount of insurance you need should be a breeze.

4. Complete the Life Insurance Checklist exercise.

Legal Documents

5. Look into a living will, durable power of attorney, and will, and tech plan. Find a password manager and online backup system to keep your digital life organized.

6. Complete Collect Your Legal Documents exercise.

Need More Help?

7. Decide if you need a professional financial advisor to help you on your journey. If you aren't sure, go to www.yearoff.co to learn how to find a quality financial planner.

Accountability Partner

8. Schedule an appointment with your AP to discuss each of these topics, and make a plan for setting up all the pieces of your safety network.

CHAPTER 9

Living Like You Have Something to Look Forward To

Every Sunday night, Megan would lie awake in bed for hours, dreading the start of another workweek. She had been a Registered Nurse for about twelve years, and the profession had been good to her. It paid well, jobs were always available, and the flexibility to work part-time while raising her kids had been ideal.

But these days, she was enjoying her career much less than she used to. After devoting six years of college and most of her adult life to nursing, Megan didn't know what to do. For some reason, she just couldn't force herself to work anymore and didn't know what to do next.

Everything looked great on paper. Her husband had a good job, and they were using her income to send their kids to a nice school and take a few vacations a year. She had recently taken a liking to $25 bottles of wine, leaving her past habit of unwinding at night with a $9 special. Would she have to change her lifestyle, she wondered?

We did the math and decided Megan could afford to leave her job. And that's not all. In that conversation, Megan confessed that she was excited to start a new business in a whole new career area. Her year off didn't take long to ramp up, and within weeks, she was off and running on her new venture.

Today, two years later, Megan is a successful interior designer who is in demand designing high-end homes in her city and filling her clients' houses with pillows. During her break, she learned how to start a business, market her services, price her expertise appropriately, and manage her time efficiently. This personal growth has carried over into her marriage and her role as a mother, and she is an inspiration to her friends and family. She feels relief every morning when she wakes up, knowing that she gets to spend her day helping people feel better about their homes.

Transitioning her life into a more meaningful way to spend her day didn't require magic. It only required action. She was able to make the leap largely because of her supportive (and attractive) husband, but if she hadn't mustered the courage to make a huge change that others might not consider "sensible," it never would have happened.

With her success, my wife Megan has inspired me to make a change as well. I love helping well-intentioned people organize their finances, but not as much as I like helping people get free of whatever is holding them back from living a life full of meaning. That's where I find profound meaning.

There is nothing special about our situation. We didn't win the lottery, we aren't so insanely smart or talented that we could skip the hard work it takes to master a skill and prepare for a year off. (My wife may be, but I'm not.) We focused on our habits every day until our progress was unstoppable.

And when you do the same, you can too.

True Risk Is Avoiding Change

So many of us are afraid to pursue the dreams we want to accomplish. Too many people without dreams are afraid to discover them. The fear feels warranted because change is scary and other people may be depending on you to be the same old you.

I would argue that making a change isn't what's scary; keeping the status quo is. As the months and years fly by, doing nothing can leave you wondering why you aren't changing, why you aren't doing anything differently. The reason is because your definition of risk is messed up. Risk isn't making an unfamiliar, unproven change; it's waking up when you're eighty and realizing you never took a shot at anything important.

Take a long look at your current situation and ask yourself one question: Is it a bigger risk for me to make a change, or to change nothing?

Help Yourself So You Can Help Others

We both know that there is more to life than money, but you can't prove money isn't important to you by ignoring it. There is also more to life than brushing your teeth, but you have (hopefully) built a habit to deal with that unpleasant chore every day. In my experience, people who avoid the topic entirely tend to be afraid of money. But if you want to make sure that money and material positions don't run your life, you need to put money front and center, at least for a while.

We all understand why airlines tell you to put on your own oxygen mask before helping others: if you pass out, you and the others are in trouble. When you set yourself up well first, you can help others for as long as it takes.

Beginning with yourself may feel selfish, but it's not. It's leading by example. It's putting your money where your mouth is. And, ultimately, it's being selfless. Nobody wants a disorganized person living paycheck to paycheck telling them how to live their life. Nobody believes an out-of-shape gym teacher. Who trusts a skinny chef?

To be that solid, organized, financially steady person who can help others, follow the steps I laid out for you in this book. If you were too excited to do the exercises this time around, now's the time to go back and fill in your answers! Then, connect with your accountability partner to review all the ways you're preparing for your year off and everything you plan to achieve. Make a plan to keep in touch throughout the year to help keep you grounded, focused, and on track.

The sooner you do the work to calculate your current and future financial situation and set up your own Year Off Money System, the more equipped you'll be to set a good financial example for your family and friends . . . and the closer you'll be to your year of freedom.

Chapter 9 Accountability
CHECKLIST

Keep Moving Forward

1. Give yourself permission to risk change.

2. Commit to keeping yourself and your money on track so you're able to help others.

Accountability Partner

3. Make a plan with your AP to stay connected!

Conclusion

Congratulations! You've made it through the book, you've implemented the Year Off Money System, and you're on your way to . . . whatever you want. Living however you want. Testing out your dream, changing careers. Making your life better.

Go big or go small, but go somewhere. Don't keep your plans a secret—tell your friends and family that you are making a change. If they don't like it now, they will eventually. Buy them this book and dare them to question your plans (and listen to reasonable suggestions). Maybe you can find someone to come with you on your journey.

In the meantime, you have an online community at your fingertips ready to support your vision of what you want your life to be. Others have taken this journey before you and are happy to share their ups and downs with you. Connect with others in your situation and motivate each other to keep moving at all costs!

Last, and hopefully not least, I will be here as well. Find me online, in print, or in person. I am here to answer your questions and develop resources to turn your vague ideas into realities that will change your community and mine for the better. Let me know what you need to keep moving!

Most people die with a surplus of untapped potential, leaving a minimal legacy behind. Until that equation is reversed, I will make myself available to encourage and support you. I will be here to take heat from all of the haters who think you're crazy so you can lie on your deathbed with no regrets, content that you gave it all you had.

Finally, keep me updated on your progress! I wish you the best of luck, but I believe that if you follow the steps in this book, you won't need it. Now is the time to unleash the real you on the world, to show yourself and everyone else what you are fully capable of. And I think we are both looking forward to seeing that.

Sincerely,
Steve Larsen

Made in the USA
Las Vegas, NV
08 April 2021